JUMP Math
Book 6 Part 1 of 2

Contents

jump math™

MULTIPLYING POTENTIAL.

JUMP Math
One Yonge Street, Suite 1014
Toronto, Ontario M5E 1E5
Canada
www.jumpmath.org

Writers: Dr. Anna Klebanov, Dr. Sohrab Rahbar, Dr. Sindi Sabourin
Editors: Megan Burns, Liane Tsui, Natalie Francis, Lindsay Karpenko, Daniel Polowin,
        Susan Bindernagel, Janice Dyer, Dawn Hunter, Leanne Rancourt, Jodi Rauch
Layout and Illustrations: Linh Lam, Fely Guinasao-Fernandes, Sawyer Paul,
        Marijke Friesen, Huy Lam, Ilyana Martinez
Cover Design: Blakeley Words+Pictures
Cover Photograph: © Marc Dietrich/Shutterstock

ISBN 978-1-928134-95-4

Second printing June 2019

Printed and bound in Canada

Welcome to JUMP Math

Entering the world of JUMP Math means believing that every child has the capacity to be fully numerate and to love math. Founder and mathematician John Mighton has used this premise to develop his innovative teaching method. The resulting resources isolate and describe concepts so clearly and incrementally that everyone can understand them.

JUMP Math is comprised of Teacher Resources, Digital Lesson Slides, student Assessment & Practice Books, assessment tools, outreach programs, and professional development. All of this is presented on the JUMP Math website: **www.jumpmath.org**.

The Teacher Resource is available on the website for free use. Read the introduction to the Teacher Resource before you begin using these materials. This will ensure that you understand both the philosophy and the methodology of JUMP Math. The Assessment & Practice Books are designed for use by students, with adult guidance. Each student will have unique needs and it is important to provide the student with the appropriate support and encouragement as he or she works through the material.

Allow students to discover the concepts by themselves as much as possible. Mathematical discoveries can be made in small, incremental steps. The discovery of a new step is like untangling the parts of a puzzle. It is exciting and rewarding.

Students will need to answer the questions marked with a ▤ in a notebook. Grid paper notebooks should always be on hand for answering extra questions or when additional room for calculation is needed.

Contents

Unit 5: Measurement: Length, Perimeter, and Mass

Unit 6: Geometry: Angles, Polygons, and Symmetry

Unit 7: Number Sense: Divisibility and Prime Numbers

Unit 8: Number Sense: Fractions

PART 2
Unit 9: Number Sense: Adding and Subtracting Decimals

Unit 10: Number Sense: Multiplying and Dividing Decimals

Unit 11: Geometry: Transformations

Unit 12: Patterns and Algebra: Equations and Graphs

Unit 13: Measurement: Area

Unit 14: Number Sense: Percentages and Ratios

Unit 15: Probability and Data Management: Probability, Collecting and Analyzing Data

Unit 16: Measurement: 3-D Shapes, Volume, and Surface Area

PA6-1 Multiplication and Division

When you make equal groups, you can write a repeated addition equation and a multiplication equation.

For example, you can group an array by rows or by columns.

group by rows

group by columns

$4 + 4 + 4 = 12$
$3 \times 4 = 12$

$3 + 3 + 3 + 3 = 12$
$4 \times 3 = 12$

1. Write two addition equations and two multiplication equations for the array.

a) ● ● ● ● ●
   ● ● ● ● ●

   $\underline{2 + 2 + 2 + 2 + 2 = 10}$

   $\underline{5 \times 2 = 10}$

   $\underline{5 + 5 = 10}$

   $\underline{2 \times 5 = 10}$

b) ● ● ● ● ●
   ● ● ● ● ●
   ● ● ● ● ●

   $3+3+3+3+3=15$
   $5 \times 5 = 15$
   $5+5+5=15$
   $3 \times 5 = 15$

c) ● ● ●
   ● ● ●
   ● ● ●
   ● ● ●

   $4+4+4=12$
   $3 \times 4 = 12$

2. Show how to find the product on the number line.

   a) Show 4×3 using 4 jumps of size 3.

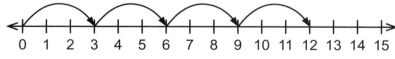

   $4 \times 3 = \underline{\quad 12 \quad}$

   b) Show 7×2 using 7 jumps of size 2.

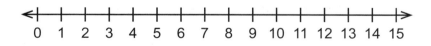

   $7 \times 2 = \underline{\qquad}$

3. John skip counts by 7s. Use John's skip counting to multiply by 7.

   a) $3 \times 7 = \underline{\qquad}$

   b) $8 \times 7 = \underline{\qquad}$

   c) $9 \times 7 = \underline{\qquad}$

   d) $5 \times 7 = \underline{\qquad}$

   e) $10 \times 7 = \underline{\qquad}$

   f) $7 \times 7 = \underline{\qquad}$

4. Answer the questions to complete the table.

		What are the objects?	What are the sets?	How many sets?	How many in each set?	How many altogether?
a)	24 toys 3 toys for each person 8 people	toys	people	8	3	24
b)	6 children 30 peanuts 5 peanuts for each child					
c)	24 roses 3 bunches of roses 8 roses in each bunch					
d)	8 tomato plants 56 tomatoes 7 tomatoes on each plant					
e)	4 canoes 3 people in each canoe 12 people					

5. Write a repeated addition equation and a multiplication equation for the situation.

a) 3 cars

   5 people in each car

   15 people altogether

   _____

   _____

b) 5 pizzas

   4 slices in each pizza

   20 slices altogether

   _____

   _____

6. Yu has 2 books. Ed has four times as many books. How many books does Ed have? _____

7. A magnifying glass makes objects look three times as big.

a) How long would a 5 cm long caterpillar look? _____ cm

b) How long would a 4 mm long ant look? _____ mm

8. Write two multiplication equations and two division equations for the situation.

9 vans

8 people in each van   _____   _____

72 people altogether   _____   _____

9. Divide $15 \div 3$ in two ways.

a) How many groups of size 3 do you need to make 15?

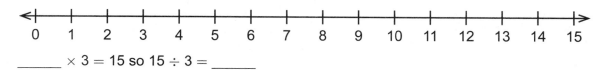

_____ $\times\ 3 = 15$ so $15 \div 3 =$ _____

b) If you divide 15 objects among 3 groups, how many go into each group? Cross out each triangle as you put it into a group.

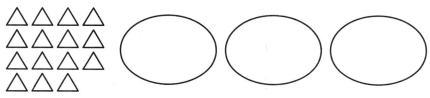

$3 \times$ _____ $= 15$ so $15 \div 3 =$ _____

10. Use the completed part of the multiplication chart to fill in the empty squares. Then answer the questions.

×	1	2	3	4	5	6	7	8	9
1	1	2	3	4	5	6	7	8	9
2		4	6	8	10	12	14	16	18
3			9	12	15	18	21	24	27
4				16	20	24	28	32	36
5					25	30	35	40	45
6						36	42	48	54
7							49	56	63
8								64	72
9									81

a) $5 \times 7 =$ _____

b) $7 \times 8 =$ _____

c) $6 \times$ _____ $= 30$

d) $30 \div 6 =$ _____

e) _____ $\times\ 8 = 24$

f) $24 \div 8 =$ _____

g) $24 \div$ _____ $= 6$

h) _____ $\div\ 4 = 9$

i) $7 \times 7 =$ _____

j) $64 \div 8 =$ _____

k) _____ $\div\ 6 = 7$

l) $72 \div$ _____ $= 9$

When 4 people share 14 almonds, each person gets 3 almonds. There are 2 leftover almonds.

        $14 \div 4 = 3 \text{ R } 2$

11. Share the almonds as equally as possible. Draw a picture and write a division equation.

a) 3 people share 7 almonds

   $\underline{7 \div 3 = 2 \text{ R } 1}$

b) 3 people share 14 almonds

   _____

c) 5 people share 11 almonds

   _____

d) 3 people share 15 almonds

   _____

12. Use $42 \div 5 = 8 \text{ R } 2$ to answer the question.

a) A shirt costs $5. John has $42. How many shirts can he buy?

b) Forty-two people go on a camping trip. Each car holds 5 people. How many cars are needed?

c) Megan has 42 hockey cards. She makes gift bags of 5 hockey cards each. She keeps the leftover hockey cards. How many hockey cards does she keep?

13. Twenty-three people are going on a family trip. Each car holds 5 people.

a) How many cars are needed?

b) If they fill up as many cars as they can, how many people will be in the car that is not full?

14. Five families are going on a camping trip. Each family has 4 people.

a) How many people are going on the trip?

b) Each canoe holds 3 people. How many canoes will they need?

c) Each canoe rental costs $5. They have $32. Do they have enough money for the canoes they will need? If so, how much do they have leftover? If not, how much more do they need?

15. A baseball pitcher pitches every 5th game. In a season of 48 games, what is the greatest number of games in which the pitcher can pitch?

BONUS ▶ How many people can share 21 grapes as equally as possible so that one is left over? Find five different answers.

Patterns and Algebra 6-1

PA6-2 Repeating Patterns

1. The **core** of a pattern is the part that repeats. Karen makes the core of several repeating patterns using red blocks (**R**) and yellow blocks (**Y**). Continue her pattern by writing Rs and Ys.

   a)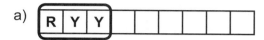

   b)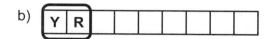

   c)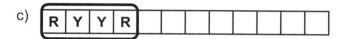

   d)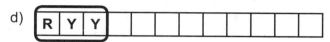

   e)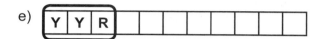

   f)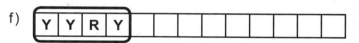

2. Write a division equation to match the picture.

   a)

   _9_ ÷ _4_ = _2_ R _1_

   b)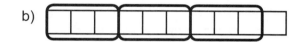

   ____ ÷ ____ = ____ R ____

   c)

   ____ ÷ ____ = ____ R ____

   d)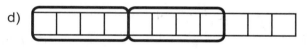

   ____ ÷ ____ = ____ R ____

3. The core is given. Extend the pattern. Circle the core as many times as it occurs. Then write a division equation to match a picture.

   a)

   _10_ ÷ _3_ = _3_ R _1_

   b)

   ____ ÷ ____ = ____ R ____

   c)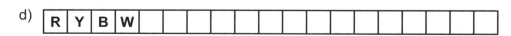

   ____ ÷ ____ = ____ R ____

   d) R Y B W

   ____ ÷ ____ = ____ R ____

4. **a)** Extend the pattern to find the 12th term.

i)
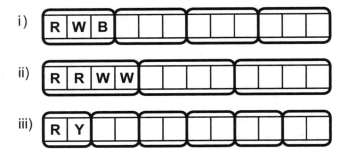

ii)

iii)

iv)

b) Make a prediction: What is the 12th term of the pattern with core RYWY? _____

Jun predicts the 12th and 14th terms of the pattern with core R R Y W as follows:

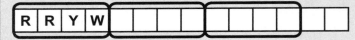

$12 \div 4 = 3$ R **0**, so the 12th term is the **last** term of the **3rd** core.

$14 \div 4 = 3$ R **2**

There are **3** cores before the 14th term. The 14th term is the **2nd** term of the next core.

The 12th term is W (white) and the 14th term is R (red).

5. Use division to predict the colour of the given block.

a) 19th block

Colour: _____

b) 35th block

Colour: _____

c) 48th block

Colour: _____

d) 100th block

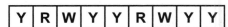

Colour: _____

6. **a)** Will the 42nd triangle in this pattern point up or down? _____

b) In what direction will the 41st arrow point? _____

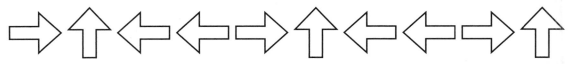

PA6-3 Extending Patterns

1. The pattern below was made by adding 3 to each term to get the next term.

    4, 7, 10, 13, 16, …

    a) Write the next three terms of the pattern. _____, _____, _____

    b) What is the 8th term of the pattern? _____

2. Add, subtract, multiply, or divide to extend the sequence.

    a) add 4   41, 45, _____, _____, _____

    b) subtract 3   25, 22, _____, _____, _____

    c) add 11   20, 31, _____, _____, _____

    d) multiply by 2 13, 26, _____, _____, _____

    e) divide by 3   81, 27, _____, _____, _____

3. Extend the sequence to find the 7th term.

    a) add 1   4, 5, 6, 7, _____

    b) subtract 2   100, 98, 96, _____

    c) add 10   30, 40, 50, 60, 70, _____

    d) multiply by 2 2, 4, 8, 16, _____

    e) divide by 10   70 000 000, 7 000 000, 700 000, 70 000, _____

4. Extend the sequence. Which term is equal to 64?

    a) multiply by 2 1, 2, 4, 8, _____   64 is the _____ term.

    b) add 10   4, 14, 24, 34, _____   64 is the _____ term.

    c) add 8   8, 16, 24, 32, _____   64 is the _____ term.

BONUS ▶ Extend the pattern.

    a) Some terms are added and some are subtracted.

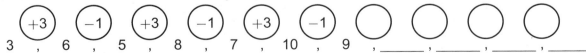

    b) Some terms are multiplied and some are subtracted.

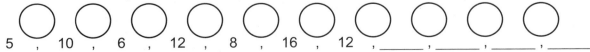

5. The pattern 3, 7, 15, … was made by doubling each term and adding 1 to get the next term.

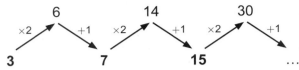

   a) Write the next three terms of the pattern. _____, _____, _____

   b) What is the 7th term of the pattern? _____

6. Repeat the two operations to extend the sequence that starts with 4.

   a) multiply by 2 and add 3

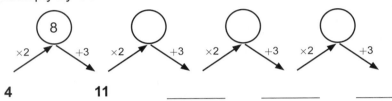

   b) multiply by 3 and subtract 1

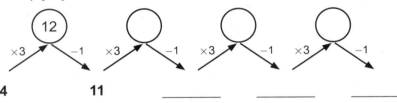

7. Extend the pattern until you reach the 5th term.

   a) add 6   3, 9, _____

   b) multiply by 3   3, 9, _____

   c) multiply by 2 and add 3   3, 9, _____

8. a) Extend the pattern until you reach 79.

   i) multiply by 2 and add 1   4, 9, _____

   ii) add 10   29, 39, _____

   iii) multiply by 3 and add 4   1, 7, _____

   b) Which pattern reaches 79 first? _____

BONUS ▶ Extend a sequence that starts "3, 5" two different ways. Describe how you
   get each next term.

   3, 5, _____   _____

   3, 5, _____   _____

PA6-4 Pattern Rules

1. What number was added to make the sequence?

   a) 12, 17, 22, 27   add __5__   b) 32, 35, 38, 41   add _____

   c) 28, 34, 40, 46   add _____   d) 50, 57, 64, 71   add _____

   e) 101, 106, 111, 116   add _____   f) 269, 272, 275, 278   add _____

2. What number was subtracted to make the sequence?

   a) 58, 56, 54, 52   subtract __2__   b) 75, 70, 65, 60   subtract _____

   c) 20, 19, 18, 17   subtract _____   d) 91, 88, 85, 82   subtract _____

   e) 67, 61, 55, 49   subtract _____   f) 900, 800, 700, 600   subtract _____

3. What do you multiply by to make the sequence?

   a) 2, 6, 18, 54   multiply by _____   b) 3, 6, 12, 24   multiply by _____

   c) 5, 20, 80, 320   multiply by _____   d) 5, 15, 45, 135   multiply by _____

4. What do you divide by to make the sequence?

   a) 120, 60, 30, 15   divide by _____   b) 189, 63, 21, 7   divide by _____

   c) 2000, 200, 20, 2   divide by _____   d) 125, 25, 5, 1   divide by _____

5. How do you get each term from the previous term?

   a) 8, 11, 14, 17   __add 3__   b) 81, 79, 77, 75   _____

   c) 3, 12, 48, 192   _____   d) 2, 10, 50, 250   _____

   e) 46, 41, 36, 31   _____   f) 4000, 400, 40, 4   _____

6. Ella says she made a pattern by adding 4 each time. Write the first three terms for two different patterns she could have made.

   Pattern 1: _____, _____, _____   Pattern 2: _____, _____, _____

7. Sara says she made a pattern starting at 4. Write the first three terms for two different patterns she could have made.

   Pattern 1: _____, _____, _____   Pattern 2: _____, _____, _____

8. John says he made a pattern by starting at 3 and adding 5 each time. Write the first three terms of John's pattern.

   _____, _____, _____

A **pattern rule** tells you how to make a pattern. For some patterns, you can make a pattern rule by saying:

- how to start the pattern and
- how to get each term from the term before it.

9. Use the first three terms in the pattern to find the rule. Then write the next term.

   a) 52, 57, 62, __67__   The rule is: ___*Start at 52 and add 5 each time.*___

   b) 3, 9, 27, _____   The rule is: _____

   c) 78, 75, 72, _____   The rule is: _____

   d) 64, 32, 16, _____   The rule is: _____

10. Use the pattern rule to make the pattern. Write the first five terms.

   a) Start at 8 and subtract 1 each time.   _____, _____, _____, _____, _____

   b) Start at 3 and multiply by 2 each time.   _____, _____, _____, _____, _____

   c) Start at 5 and add 6 each time.   _____, _____, _____, _____, _____

   d) Start at 81 and divide by 3 each time.   _____, _____, _____, _____, _____

11. Find the given term in the pattern.

   a) Start at 36 and add 12 each time.   Rough Work:

      The third term is __60__.   *36, 48, 60*_____

   b) Start at 32 and divide by 2 each time.

      The fourth term is _____.   _____

   c) Start at 50 and subtract 4 each time.

      The eighth term is _____.   _____

   d) Start at 2 and multiply by 4 each time.

      The third term is _____.   _____

12. Which term in the pattern is equal to 18?   Rough work:

   a) Start at 3 and add 5 each time. __4th__   *3, 8, 13, 18*_____

   b) Start at 2 and multiply by 3 each time. _____   _____

   c) Start at 88 and subtract 10 each time. _____ _____

13. The first term is missing. Fill it in.

   a) _____, 7, 10, 13, 16   b) _____, 98, 96, 94, 92   c) _____, 6, 18, 54, 162

14. A plant that is 17 cm tall grows 2 cm each week.

a) Continue the sequence.

17, _____, _____, _____
  1 week   2 weeks   3 weeks

b) How tall will the plant be after three weeks? _____

c) After how many weeks will the plant be 27 cm tall? _____

15. Make a pattern to solve the problem.

a) Hanna has $49. She spends $8 each day. How much money does she have left after 5 days?

Make the pattern: 49, _41_ , _33_ , _25_ , _17_ , _9_

Answer the question: _She has $9 left after 5 days._

b) Matt has a roll of 74 stamps. He uses 7 stamps each day for 4 days. How many stamps are left?

Make the pattern: 74, _____, _____, _____, _____

Answer the question: _____

c) Six people start a new town. Every 20 years, the population doubles. After how many years will the town have more than 100 people?

Make the pattern: _____

Answer the question: _____

d) Ava has $30. She makes $8 an hour cutting lawns. She wants to buy a sweater that costs $86. How many hours does she have to work?

Make the pattern: _____

Answer the question: _____

e) Ronin has saved $49. He spends $8 each day. How much money does he have left after 5 days?

f) Yu has a roll of 113 stamps. She uses 8 each day for 7 days. How many are left?

g) Glen has $2000 at home. Every day, he donates half of his money to a different charity until he has less than $200. He spends the rest. How much money does he spend?

PA6-5 Tables of Values

Cody creates an **increasing pattern** with squares. He records the number of squares in each figure in a table of values. He also records the number of squares he adds each time he makes a new figure.

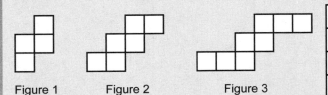

Figure	# of Squares
1	4
2	6
3	8

Figure 1　　Figure 2　　Figure 3

2 ← Number of squares
2 ← added each time

The number of squares in the figures are 4, 6, 8, ….

Cody writes a rule for this number pattern:

Start at 4 and add 2 each time.

1. Cody makes other increasing patterns with squares.

   How many squares does he add to make each new figure?

   Write your answer in the circles. Then write a rule for the pattern.

a)

Figure	Number of Squares
1	2
2	8
3	14

Rule:

b)

Figure	Number of Squares
1	3
2	9
3	15

Rule:

c)

Figure	Number of Squares
1	1
2	6
3	11

Rule:

d)

Figure	Number of Squares
1	1
2	8
3	15

Rule:

e)

Figure	Number of Squares
1	5
2	13
3	21

Rule:

f)

Figure	Number of Squares
1	11
2	22
3	33

Rule:

2. Extend the number pattern.

a)

Figure	Number of Squares
1	2
2	10
3	18

b)

Figure	Number of Squares
1	4
2	9
3	14

c)

Figure	Number of Squares
1	7
2	11
3	15

3. After making Figure 3, Cody has only 35 squares left. Does he have enough squares to complete Figure 4? Circle your answer.

a)

Figure	Number of Squares
1	4
2	13
3	22

Yes   No

b)

Figure	Number of Squares
1	6
2	17
3	28

Yes   No

c)

Figure	Number of Squares
1	9
2	17
3	25

Yes   No

4. Make a table of values to show which figure in the pattern will need 15 shapes.

a)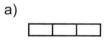

b)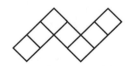

5. Make a table of values for the first four terms.

a) Start at 5. To get the next term, double the number and subtract 2.

b) Start at 5. To get the next term, subtract 2 and double the result.

c) Start at 5. To get the next term, double the number and add 4.

d) Start at 5. To get the next term, add 2 and double the result.

6. In Question 5, which two parts resulted in the same pattern? _____ and _____

7. a) The snow is 17 cm deep at 5 p.m.
Each hour, 4 cm of snow falls.
How deep is the snow at 9 p.m.?

Time	Depth of Snow
5 p.m.	17 cm

b) Jin had $42 in savings by the end of July.
Each month he saves $9. How much will he have by the end of October?

Month	Savings
July	$42

8. Sara's fish tank is leaking.
At 6 p.m. there are 21 L of water in the tank.
At 7 p.m. there are 18 L, and at 8 p.m. there are 15 L.

a) How many litres of water leak out each hour?

_____

b) How many litres will be left in the tank at 10 p.m.?

_____

c) How many hours will it take for all the water to leak out?

_____

Time	Amount of Water in the Tank
6 p.m.	21 L
7 p.m.	18 L
8 p.m.	15 L
9 p.m.	
10 p.m.	

9. A store rents snowboards at $7 for the first hour and $5 for every hour after that.

a) How much does it cost to rent a snowboard for 3 hours?

b) John has $42. How many hours can he rent a snowboard for?

10. a) How many triangles would Marko need to make a figure with 10 squares?

Figure 1   Figure 2   Figure 3

b) Avril says that she needs 15 triangles to make the sixth figure. Is she correct? Explain.

11. Marla saves $55 in August. She saves $6 each month after that. Alex saves $42 in August.
He saves $7 each month after that. Who will have saved the most money by the end of January?

PA6-6 Variables

1. Replace the changing quantity with the letter n.

a) $1 + 5 \quad 2 + 5 \quad 3 + 5$
b) $2 \times 5 \quad 2 \times 6 \quad 2 \times 7$
c) $8 - 1 \quad 8 - 2 \quad 8 - 3$

<u> $n + 5$ </u>
   _____
   _____

A **variable** is a letter or symbol (such as w, T, or h) that represents a number.

To make an **algebraic expression**, replace some numbers in a **numerical expression** with variables.

Examples of numerical expressions:	$7 + 1$	4×9	$(2 + 6) - (3 \times 5)$
Examples of algebraic expressions:	$w + 1$	$4 \times T$	$(2 + t) - (3 \times h)$

---

2. Write an expression for the distance a car would travel at the speed and in the time given.

a) Speed: 60 km per hour
   Time: 3 hours
   Distance: <u> 60×3 </u> km

b) Speed: 50 km per hour
   Time: 4 hours
   Distance: _____ km

c) Speed: 70 km per hour
   Time: h hours
   Distance: _____ km

In the product of a number and a variable, the multiplication sign is usually not written.

$3 \times T$ can be written as $3T$ and $5 \times z$ can be written as $5z$.

---

3. Renting skis costs \$5 an hour. Write a numerical expression for the cost of renting skis for…

a) h hours: <u> $5 \times h$ </u> or <u> $5h$ </u>
b) t hours: _____ or _____

RENT SKIS
\$5 an hour

c) x hours: _____ or _____
d) n hours: _____ or _____

When replacing a variable with a number, use brackets.

Example: Replacing n with 7 in the expression $3n$ gives $3(7)$, which is another way to write 3×7.

---

4. Write the number 2 in the brackets and evaluate.

a) $5(2) = $ <u> 5×2 </u> $= $ <u> 10 </u>
b) $3(\quad) = $ _____ $= $ _____
c) $4(\quad) = $ _____ $= $ _____

5. Replace the variable with the given number and then evaluate.

a) $2h, \quad h = 3$
   $2(3) = 6$

b) $n + 2, \quad n = 5$

c) $4t, \quad t = 6$

d) $h \div 3, \quad h = 21$

e) $7 - z, \quad z = 2$

f) $6 + m, \quad m = 4$

PA6-7 Finding Rules—One Operation

In a theatre, the number of chairs in a row is always 4 greater than the row number.

row number $+ 4 =$ number of chairs (or $r + 4 = c$ for short)

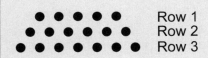

Row 1
Row 2
Row 3

Row (r)	$r + 4 = c$	Chairs (c)
1	$1 + 4 = 5$	5
2	$2 + 4 = 6$	6
3	$3 + 4 = 7$	7

1. Each table represents a different arrangement of chairs. Complete the tables.

a)

Row (r)	$r + 6 = c$	Chairs (c)
1		
2		
3		

b)

Row (r)	$r + 24 = c$	Chairs (c)
1		
2		
3		

2. Complete the table for the arrangement of chairs. Then write an equation.

a)

Row 1
Row 2
Row 3

Row (r)	Chairs (c)

_____

b)

Row 1
Row 2
Row 3

Row (r)	Chairs (c)

_____

c)

Row 1
Row 2
Row 3

Row (r)	Chairs (c)

_____

3. Apply the rule to the input numbers to get the output numbers.

a) Add 4 to the input.

Input	Output
1	
2	
3	

b) Multiply the input by 6.

Input	Output
2	
6	
9	

c) Divide the input by 4.

Input	Output
40	
24	
48	

A **formula** is an equation that tells you how to get the **output numbers** (*B*) from the **input numbers** (*A*). In a formula, you write the output number first.

Example: If the rule is "multiply the input by 6," the formula is $B = 6 \times A$ or $B = 6A$.

4. Write a formula that tells you how to get the output numbers (*B*) from the input numbers (*A*).

a)

A	B
1	2
2	4
3	6
4	8

Rule: _multiply by 2_

Formula: _$B = 2A$_

b)

A	B
1	6
2	7
3	8
4	9

Rule: _____

Formula: _____

c)

A	B
1	0
2	1
3	2
4	3

Rule: _____

Formula: _____

d)

A	B
3	1
9	3
15	5
21	7

Rule: _____

Formula: _____

e)

A	B
80	8
50	5
700	70
1900	190

Rule: _____

Formula: _____

f)

A	B
8	40
9	45
6	30
10	50

Rule: _____

Formula: _____

5. The formula tells you how to get the output number (*B*) from the input number (*A*). Write the rule in words.

a) $B = 3A$ Rule: _multiply the input by 3_

b) $B = A - 4$ Rule: _____

c) $B = A + 2$ Rule: _____

6. Write a formula to get the number of chairs from the number of tables. Say what variables you are using for the number of chairs and tables.

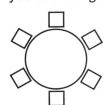 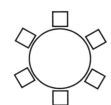 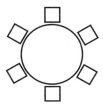

Let _____ be the number of chairs.

Let _____ be the number of tables.

Formula: _____

7. Complete the table of values. Then write a formula that tells you how to get the second number from the first number.

a)

Vertical Lines (v)	Horizontal lines (h)
1	3

Formula:

$h =$

b)

Suns (s)	Moons (m)

Formula:

$m =$

c)

Stars (s)	Diamonds (d)

Formula:

d)

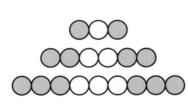

Grey circles (g)	White circles (w)

Formula:

8. A pattern was made from hexagons and triangles.

Figure 1

Figure 2

Figure 3

a) Draw a table, then write a formula for how to get the number of triangles from the number of hexagons.

b) How many triangles are needed for 9 hexagons in the pattern? How do you know?

9. Draw a pattern in which the formula $t = 4s$ shows how to get the number of triangles (*t*) from the number of squares (*s*).

PA6-8 Two Types of Pattern Rules

1. Complete the table by following the rule.

a) Multiply the term number by 2.

Term Number	Term Value
1	
2	
3	
4	

b) Start at 1 and add 2 each time.

Term Number	Term Value
1	
2	
3	
4	

c) Start at 2 and add 2 each time.

Term Number	Term Value
1	
2	
3	
4	

2. Which two rules in Question 1 made the same pattern?

Parts _____ and _____

There are two types of pattern rules:

1. Rules that tell you how to extend the sequence.

2. Rules that use a formula to get each term from the term number.

Example: 2, 4, 6, 8, 10, …

Start at 2 and add 2 each time.

Multiply the term number by 2.

3. Complete the table.

	Pattern	Rule to extend the sequence	Rule using a formula
a)	3, 4, 5, 6, 7, …	Start at 3 and add 1 each time.	Add 2 to the term number.
b)	3, 6, 9, 12, 15, …		
c)	8, 9, 10, 11, 12, …		
d)			Multiply the term number by 5.
e)		Start at 10 and add 10 each time.	
f)			Add 4 to the term number.

4. The picture shows how a banquet hall seats people around its rectangular tables.

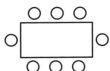 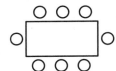 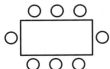

a) Make a table of values that shows the number of tables and the number of people.

Number of Tables	Number of Chairs

b) Write two rules for how to get the number of chairs.

   i)   Rule to extend the pattern: _____

   ii) Rule to get the number of chairs (C) from the number of tables (T): _____

c) If the banquet hall has 50 tables, how many people can it seat? Did you extend the pattern or did you use a formula? Explain your choice.

_____

_____

_____

5. Sun makes a pattern using squares.

              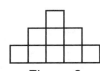

Figure 1   Figure 2   Figure 3   Figure 4

a) Draw Figure 4.

b) Complete the sequence that shows the number of squares in each figure. Start by writing the gaps in the circles. Then extend the pattern in the gaps to extend the sequence.

   __1__ , __4__ , __9__ , _____ , _____ , _____
   Figure 1   Figure 2   Figure 3   Figure 4   Figure 5   Figure 6

c) Predict how many squares are in the 10th figure. Use the multiplication chart and the table provided.

Figure 1	Figure 2	Figure 3	Figure 4
__1__ × __1__	__2__ × __2__	____ × ____	____ × ____

×	1	2	3	4
1	1	2	3	4
2	2	4	6	8
3	3	6	9	12
4	4	8	12	16

I predict the 10th figure will have _____ squares

because _____ .

NS6-1 Place Value

hundred thousands   ten thousands   thousands

$$8\;3\;1\;7\;5\;2\;4$$

millions   hundreds   tens   ones

1. Write the place value of the underlined digit.

a) 56 2<u>3</u>6 | *tens* |

b) <u>1</u> 956 336 | |

c) 8 2<u>5</u>6 601 | |

d) 7 103 25<u>6</u> | |

e) 2 5<u>8</u>9 143 | |

f) 3 <u>9</u>21 052 | |

g) 903 <u>7</u>46 | |

h) 2 6<u>0</u>5 416 | |

2. Underline the digit 5 in the number. Write the place value of the digit 5 in the number.

a) 3<u>5</u> 689 | *thousands* |

b) 5 308 603 | |

c) 36 905 | |

d) 512 | |

e) 2542 | |

f) 3 451 628 | |

g) 43 251 | |

h) 152 776 | |

i) 1 543 001 | |

j) 5 704 021 | |

k) 7305 | |

l) 9 695 000 | |

3. Write the number into the place value chart.

	Millions	Hundred Thousands	Ten Thousands	Thousands	Hundreds	Tens	Ones
a) 2 316 953							
b) 62 507							
c) 5 604 891							
d) 1399							
e) 17							
f) 998 260							
g) 5 002 008							

The number 784 523 is a **six-digit number**.

- The **digit** 7 stands for 700 000—the **value** of the digit 7 is 700 000.
- The digit 8 stands for 80 000—the value of the digit 8 is 80 000.
- The digit 4 stands for 4000—the value of the digit 4 is 4000.
- The digit 5 stands for 500—the value of the digit 5 is 500.
- The digit 2 stands for 20—the value of the digit 2 is 20.
- The digit 3 stands for 3—the value of the digit 3 is 3.

4. Write the **value** of each digit.

a) 654 872

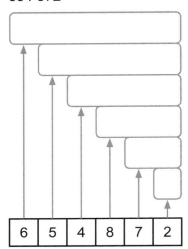

b) 128 537

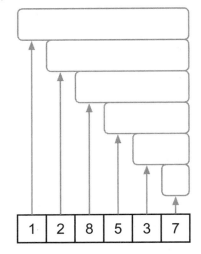

5. What does the digit 7 stand for in the number?

a) 8476

> 70

b) 38 725

c) 93 726

d) 730 025

e) 7250

f) 64 297

g) 43 075

h) 382 457

6. Fill in the blank.

a) In the number 4523, the digit 5 stands for _____.

b) In the number 34 528, the digit 3 stands for _____.

c) In the number 420 583, the value of the digit 8 is _____.

d) In the number 723 594, the digit _____ is in the ten thousands place.

BONUS ▶ In the number 2 709 926, the digit 2 stands for _____ and _____.

Number words for the tens place:	ten	twenty	thirty	forty	fifty	sixty	seventy	eighty	ninety

7. Say whether the underlined digits represent **thousands** or **millions**.

   a) <u>327</u> 510 210 _millions_   b) 216 <u>772</u> 015 _____   c) <u>5</u> 321 859 _____

   d) 879 <u>054</u> 815 _____   e) <u>129</u> 000 307 _____   f) 2 <u>500</u> 623 _____

8. Write the value of the underlined digits.

   a) <u>375</u> 231 872 _three hundred seventy-five million_ _____

   b) 287 <u>036</u> 253 _____

   c) <u>79</u> 253 812   d) 3 <u>770</u> 823   e) 22 <u>306</u> 235

9. Write numerals for the number words.

   a) Seventy-three million, fifty-seven thousand, one hundred four

   b) Nine hundred seven million, four hundred three thousand, twenty-one

10. Write number words for the numerals.

   a) 275 381 210   b) 89 023 100   c) 998 325 593

11. Write how many years ago each period started, using words and then numerals.
   (Note: "mya" means millions of years ago.)

	Dinosaurs evolve	*Birds evolve*	*Dinosaurs become extinct*
	Triassic Period	Jurassic Period	Cretaceous Period

248 mya		199 mya		145 mya		65 mya

12. a) Write the distance from each planet to the sun using words.

   b) The distance from Earth to the moon is 384 400 km. Write this distance using words.

   c) **Billions** come after millions. The planet Neptune is 4 468 640 000 km from the sun. Write this number in words.

Planet	Distance from Sun (km)
Mercury	57 600 000
Venus	107 520 000
Earth	148 640 000

13. Blood contains different kinds of cells. There are about 225 000 000 red blood cells, 335 000 white blood cells, and 12 800 000 platelets in a drop of blood. Write the numbers of different blood cells in words.

NS6-2 Representation in Expanded Form

1. Write the number in expanded form. Then draw a base ten model.

   Example: 3152 = $\boxed{3000 + 100 + 50 + 2}$

   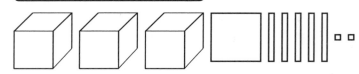

   a) 4354 = [   ]

   b) 2604 = [   ]

2. Write the number in expanded form using numerals and words.

   a) 2 536 784 = <u>2 millions + 5 hundred thousands + 3 ten thousands + 6 thousands</u>

   <u>+ 7 hundreds + 8 tens + 4 ones</u>

   b) 6 235 401 = _____

   _____

   c) 3 056 026 = _____

   _____

3. Write the number in expanded form using numerals.

   a) 72 613 = <u>70 000 + 2000 + 600 + 10 + 3</u>   b) 36 = _____

   c) 12 052 = _____   d) 526 = _____

   e) 56 384 = _____   f) 2493 = _____

   g) 3 082 385 = _____

   h) 9 340 042 = _____

4. Write the number for the expanded form.

   a) $6000 + 700 + 40 + 5 = $ _____

   b) $800 + 60 + 8 = $ _____

   c) $3000 + 30 + 2 = $ _____

   d) $50\,000 + 6000 + 400 + 90 + 3 = $ _____

   e) $30\,000 + 2000 + 500 = $ _____

   f) $90\,000 + 3000 + 600 + 8 = $ _____

   g) $70\,000 + 700 + 7 = $ _____

   h) $10\,000 + 6000 + 200 + 30 + 4 = $ _____

   i) $4\,000\,000 + 300\,000 + 20\,000 + 7000 + 800 + 50 + 2 = $ _____

   j) $2\,000\,000 + 300\,000 + 2000 + 30 + 2 = $ _____

   BONUS ▶ $300\,000 + 2\,000\,000 + 20\,000 + 70\,000 + 200 = $ _____

5. Find the missing numbers.

   a) $2000 + 600 + $ _____ $ + 5 = 2645$

   b) $4000 + 200 + $ _____ $ + 5 = 4285$

   c) $40\,000 + 3000 + $ _____ $ + 10 + 5 = 43\,715$

   d) $80\,000 + 5000 + $ _____ $ + 60 + 3 = 85\,263$

   e) $20\,000 + 6000 + 300 + $ _____ $ = 26\,302$

   f) _____ $ + 400 = 9400$

   g) $6000 + $ _____ $ = 6080$

   h) $80\,000 + $ _____ $ + $ _____ $ = 87\,005$

   i) $300\,000 + 90\,000 + $ _____ $ + $ _____ $ = 390\,702$

   j) _____ $ + 300\,000 + 10\,000 + 500 + $ _____ $ = 7\,310\,540$

   k) $9\,000\,000 + $ _____ $ + 50\,000 + $ _____ $ + 800 + $ _____ $ = 9\,458\,803$

6. How many thousands blocks would you need to represent a million? _____

7. In the number 38 562, what is the sum of the tens digit and the thousands digit?

8. a) How many two-digit numbers have digits that add to 12?

   b) How many two-digit numbers have digits that add to 10?

   c) How many two-digit numbers have digits that add to 8?

9. Using only 5 base ten blocks, make (or draw) a model of a number such that…

   a) the number is odd.

   b) there are twice as many thousands blocks as hundreds blocks.

10. Represent the number 3564 in four different ways.

   • by sketching a base ten model
   • in words
   • in expanded form (2 ways)

NS6-3 Comparing and Ordering Numbers

1. Write the number in expanded form. Then complete the sentence.

   a) 725 = __700__ + __20__ + __5__

      735 = __700__ + __30__ + __5__

      __735__ is greater than __725__.

   b) 723 = _____ + _____ + _____

      623 = _____ + _____ + _____

      _____ is greater than _____.

   c) 463 = _____ + _____ + _____

      462 = _____ + _____ + _____

      _____ is greater than _____.

   d) 309 = _____ + _____ + _____

      319 = _____ + _____ + _____

      _____ is greater than _____.

2. Circle the digits that are different in the pair of numbers. Then write the greater number in the box.

   a) 5 4 9 ⦶3⦶ 7
      5 4 9 ⦵2⦵ 7
      ┌─────────────┐
      │ 54 937   │
      └─────────────┘

   b) 9 5 4 1 0 3
      9 5 6 1 0 3
      ┌─────────────┐
      │   │
      └─────────────┘

   c) 2 5 3 2 1 1 9
      2 5 3 2 1 0 9
      ┌─────────────┐
      │   │
      └─────────────┘

   d) 4 5 0 1 8 6 2 1 4
      4 5 0 1 8 6 2 2 4
      ┌─────────────┐
      │   │
      └─────────────┘

3. Reading from left to right, circle the first digits that are different in the pair of numbers. Then write the greater number in the box.

   a) 6 4 1 5 ⦶8⦶ 3
      6 4 1 5 ⦵9⦵ 7
      ┌─────────────┐
      │ 641 597   │
      └─────────────┘

   b) 5 2 3 7 1 4
      5 2 7 3 1 4
      ┌─────────────┐
      │   │
      └─────────────┘

   c) 3 2 4 3 7 1
      4 2 4 6 1 1
      ┌─────────────┐
      │   │
      └─────────────┘

   d) 1 6 2 3 7
      1 6 2 2 7
      ┌─────────────┐
      │   │
      └─────────────┘

> "5 > 3" means "5 is greater than 3" and "3 < 5" means "3 is less than 5." The signs > and < are called **inequality signs**.

4. Write the correct inequality sign (> or <) in the box.

   a) 5392 $\boxed{>}$ 5246

   b) 23 172 $\boxed{}$ 23 157

   c) 323 728 $\boxed{}$ 323 729

   d) 6000 $\boxed{}$ 5999

   e) 152 719 $\boxed{}$ 152 620

   f) 52 305 $\boxed{}$ 61 302

   g) 3289 $\boxed{}$ 10 104

   h) 2 351 052 $\boxed{}$ 2 351 049

   i) 15 327 $\boxed{}$ 15 232

   j) 7214 $\boxed{}$ 18 932

   k) 382 636 $\boxed{}$ 382 522

   l) 2 627 382 $\boxed{}$ 2 643 927

5. Create the greatest possible *four-digit* number using the digits given. Only use each digit once.

a) 4, 3, 2, 6 _____

b) 7, 8, 9, 4 _____

c) 0, 4, 1, 2 _____

6. Create the greatest possible number using these digits. Only use each digit once.

a) 3, 4, 1, 2, 8 _____

b) 2, 8, 9, 1, 5 _____

c) 3, 6, 1, 5, 4 _____

7. Use the digits to create the greatest number, the least number, and a number in between.

	Digits	Greatest Number	Number in Between	Least Number
a)	8 5 7 2 1			
b)	2 1 5 3 9			
c)	3 0 1 5 3			

8. Arrange the numbers in order, starting with the *least* number.

a) 3257   3352   3183

_____ , _____ , _____

b) 17 251   17 385   17 256

_____ , _____ , _____

c) 87 500   87 498   87 499

_____ , _____ , _____

d) 36 725   3281   93 859

_____ , _____ , _____

e) 60 052   60 001   60 021

_____ , _____ , _____

f) 273   5891   17

_____ , _____ , _____

g) 23 809, 45 789 001, 423 010

h) 648 973 902, 973 902 648, 902 648 973

i) 301 298 456, 42 907 812, 329 564, 789 234 502

j) 72 572, 572 000, 572 000 572, 57 200 572, 572 572

9. Using the digits 0, 1, 2, 3, 4, create a number greater than 32 000 and less than 34 000.

10. Using the digits 3, 5, 6, 7, 8, create an even number greater than 85 000 and less than 87 000.

11. Which digit is covered by the black square?

a) 32 675 < 32 ■56 < 32 854

b) 68 379 < 68 ■32 < 68 464

c) 999 999 < ■ 233 458 < 2 000 000

d) 223 789 021 > 22■ 935 784 > 222 934 567

NS6-4 Addition and Subtraction

1. Write the numbers in expanded form. Then add the place values and regroup.

a)   473   _____ hundreds + _____ tens + _____ ones
   + 291   + _____ hundreds + _____ tens + _____ one
   _____
               _____ hundreds + _____ tens + _____ ones
   Regroup: _____ hundreds + _____ tens + _____ ones

b)   3418   _____ thousands + _____ hundreds + _____ ten + _____ ones
   + 2945   + _____ thousands + _____ hundreds + _____ tens + _____ ones
   _____
               _____ thousands + _____ hundreds + _____ tens + _____ ones
   Regroup: _____ thousands + _____ hundreds + _____ tens + _____ ones

2. Add. You will need to regroup.

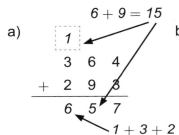

a) (see worked example: 6 + 9 = 15, 1 + 3 + 2)

```
    1
  3 6 4
+ 2 9 3
---------
  6 5 7
```

b)
```
  5 7 1
+ 2 5 5
---------
```

c)
```
  6 5 2
+   9 4
---------
```

d)
```
  3 6 2
+ 4 8 2
---------
```

3. Add. Regroup when necessary.

a)
```
  4 3 5
+ 1 2 9
---------
```

b)
```
  2 0 8
+ 3 5 7
---------
```

c)
```
  3 7 2
+ 1 7 5
---------
```

d)
```
  6 9 9
+ 2 1 4
---------
```

e)
```
  4 3 7 1
+ 1 8 2 5
-----------
```

f)
```
  2 5 0 2
+ 3 5 6 7
-----------
```

g)
```
  3 8 5 4
+ 1 8 3 5
-----------
```

h)
```
  6 9 7 9
+ 2 1 1 6
-----------
```

i)
```
  4 6 5 7
+ 1 6 3 5
-----------
```

j)
```
  2 9 4 6
+ 3 5 4 7
-----------
```

k)
```
  3 7 6 2
+ 1 9 7 5
-----------
```

l)
```
  5 9 8 9
+ 3 1 1 4
-----------
```

4. Add. Regroup when necessary.

a)
```
    1  6  8
+   3  2  3
_____
```

b)
```
    2  5  5
+   3  6  2
_____
```

c)
```
    3  9  5
+   1  2  3
_____
```

d)
```
    4  6  5
+   1  5  9
_____
```

e)
```
    4  7  5  2
+      6  3  6
_____
```

f)
```
    2  9  4  6
+         9  7
_____
```

g)
```
    8  7  5  2
+   1  0  7  5
_____
```

h)
```
    6  9  7  9
+   7  1  2  6
_____
```

i)
```
    5  8  4  6
+   1  1  3  5
_____
```

j)
```
    3  5  6  4
+   2  8  1  3
_____
```

k)
```
    7  3  2  4  6
+   1  8  3  8  2
_____
```

l)
```
    2  3  5  2  7  5
+   5  1  2  9  1  3
_____
```

5. Line up the numbers correctly in the grid. Add. Regroup when necessary.

a) 449 + 346

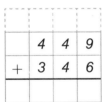

b) 273 + 456

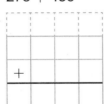

c) 347 + 72

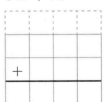

d) 16 890 + 27 325

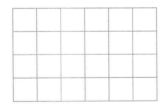

e) 91 892 + 4956

f) 345 678 + 876 543

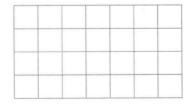

6. a) Camile cycled 2357 km one year and 5753 km the next. How many kilometres did she cycle altogether?

b) Two nearby towns have populations of 442 670 and 564 839. What is the total population of both towns?

7. Regroup 1 ten as 10 ones. Rewrite the subtraction question.

a)
```
      4  13
      5   3
  -   3   6
```

b)
```
      6   5
  -   2   9
```

c)
```
      6   7
  -   4   8
```

d)
```
      2   4   4
  -   1   3   7
```

8. Subtract. You will need to regroup once.

a)
```
      7  12
      8   2
  -   3   7
      4   5
```

b)
```
      5   4
  -   2   6
```

c)
```
      5  13
      6   3   8
  -   4   5   3
```

d)
```
      8   5   4
  -   3   7   2
```

e)
```
      7   5   5
  -   3   8   2
```

f)
```
      4   2   3
  -   1   8   2
```

g)
```
      7   8   4
  -   2   4   8
```

h)
```
      3   4   3
  -   2   1   9
```

i)
```
      2   8   2   5
  -   1   5   1   7
```

j)
```
      6   7   1   9
  -   3   1   6   4
```

k)
```
      3   2   9   8
  -   1   8   3   8
```

l)
```
      2   3   7   5
  -   1   4   7   1
```

Sometimes you need to regroup several times. When subtracting 6423 − 3746, regroup 1 ten as 10 ones, 1 hundred as 10 tens, and 1 thousand as 10 hundreds.

Example:

Step 1
```
          1  13
    6  4  2  3
  - 3  7  4  6
```

Step 2
```
          1  13
    6  4  2  3
  - 3  7  4  6
             7
```

Step 3
```
       11
       3  1  13
    6  4  2  3
  - 3  7  4  6
          7  7
```

Step 4
```
          13 11
    5  3  1  13
    6  4  2  3
  - 3  7  4  6
       6  7  7
```

Step 5
```
          13 11
    5  3  1  13
    6  4  2  3
  - 3  7  4  6
    2  6  7  7
```

9. Subtract, regrouping two or three times.

a)
```
      8   9   2   9
  -   4   9   5   8
```

b)
```
      8   7   2   5
  -   4   9   5   8
```

c)
```
      6   4   3   7
  -   2   6   7   8
```

d)
```
      4   5   6   3
  -   1   7   9   5
```

10. Subtract. Regroup when necessary.

a)

	7	8	4	3
−	4	8	6	5

b)

	1	0	0	0	0
−		6	4	8	6

c)

	4	3	0	2	4
−	3	8	3	9	2

d)

	4	0	8	5	9	1
−		2	3	7	8	4

e)

	1	0	0	0	0	0	0
−		7	8	3	6	0	8

f)

	1	0	1	0	1	0	1
−			3	4	5	6	7

11. a) File Data1.PDF contains 6497 KB of data. File Data2.PDF contains 4378 KB of data. How much data is in both files together?

b) The Falcon 9 rocket consists of two parts called stages. Stage 1 weighs 25 600 kg and its fuel weighs 395 700 kg. Stage 2 weighs 3900 kg and its fuel weighs 92 670 kg. What is the combined mass of both stages and the fuel?

12. a) The Nile River is about 6690 km long and the Amazon River is about 6440 km long. How much longer is the Nile River than the Amazon River?

b) Mars has two moons, Phobos and Deimos. The average distance from Mars is 9378 km for Phobos and 23 459 km for Deimos. How much farther from Mars on average is Deimos?

13. The table shows the shoreline length of the Great Lakes. Use the information in the table to answer the questions.

a) How much longer is the shoreline of Lake Superior than Lake Ontario?

b) Which is longer, the combined shoreline length of Lake Superior, Lake Erie, and Lake Ontario or the combined shoreline length of Lake Huron and Lake Michigan? How much longer?

c) The total shoreline length of Canada is 202 080 km. Which is longer, the total shoreline length of Canada or of the Great Lakes? How much longer?

d) Make your own addition and subtraction questions using the information in the table. Calculate the answers.

Lake	Shoreline Length (km)
Superior	4393
Huron	6164
Michigan	2639
Erie	1402
Ontario	1146

Lake Superior
Lake Huron
Lake Ontario
Lake Michigan
Lake Erie

NS6-5 Rounding

1. Draw an arrow to the 0 or 10 to show whether the circled number is closer to 0 or 10.

   a)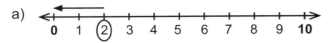

   b)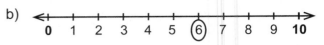

   c)

   d)

2. a) Which one-digit numbers are closer to 0? _____

   b) Which one-digit numbers are closer to 10? _____

   c) Why is 5 a special case? _____

3. For the circled number, draw an arrow to show which multiple of 10 you would round to.
   Then round the number to the nearest 10.

   a)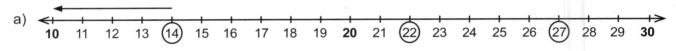

   Round to: _____10_____   _____   _____

   b)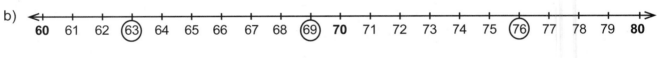

   Round to: _____   _____   _____

   c)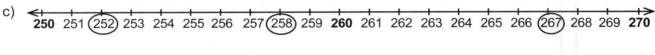

   Round to: _____   _____   _____

4. Circle the correct answer.

   a) 29 is closer to: 20 or 30

   b) 14 is closer to: 10 or 20

   c) 254 is closer to: 250 or 260

   d) 488 is closer to: 480 or 490

5. Draw an arrow to show whether the circled number is closer to 0 or 100.

   a)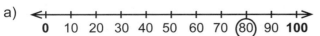

   b)

6. Is 50 closer to 0 or to 100? Why is 50 a special case?

   _____

7. Circle the correct answer.

   a) 80 is closer to: 0 or 100

   b) 20 is closer to: 0 or 100

   c) 40 is closer to: 0 or 100

   d) 60 is closer to: 0 or 100

8. Show the approximate position of the number on the line. What multiple of 100 do you round to?

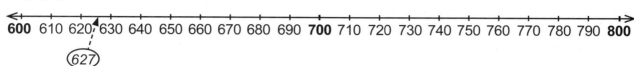

   a) 627

      Round to _____

   b) 683

      Round to _____

   c) 795

      Round to _____

   d) 706

      Round to _____

9. Circle the correct answer.

   a) 165 is closer to: 100 or 200

   b) 635 is closer to: 600 or 700

   c) 870 is closer to: 800 or 900

   d) 532 is closer to: 500 or 600

10. Draw an arrow to show whether the circled number is closer to 0 or 1000.

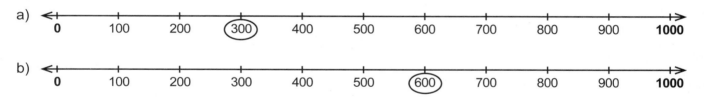

11. Circle the correct answer.

    a) 100 is closer to: 0 or 1000   b) 900 is closer to: 0 or 1000   c) 600 is closer to: 0 or 1000

12. Draw an arrow to show which multiple of 1000 you round to.

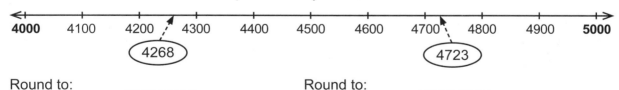

    Round to: _____   Round to: _____

13. Circle the correct answer.

    a) 2953 is closer to: 2000 or 3000

    b) 7293 is closer to: 7000 or 8000

    c) 5521 is closer to: 5000 or 6000

    d) 8232 is closer to: 8000 or 9000

14. Write a rule for rounding a four-digit number to the nearest thousand.

15. Underline the digit you want to round to. Look at the next digit. Do you round up or down?

a) thousands

2	7	3	2	5

round up
(round down)

b) ten thousands

6	8	4	1	1

round up
round down

c) hundreds

7	4	5	0	8

round up
round down

d) tens

4	0	8	1	2	3

round up
round down

e) thousands

1	9	6	7	8	2

round up
round down

f) thousands

3	0	0	5	2	7

round up
round down

Step 1: Round the underlined digit up or down.

To round up, add 1 to the digit.
To round down, keep the digit the same.

hundreds

4	5	7	3	2	5
			3		

up
(down)

Step 2: The digits to the right of the rounded digit become zeros.

The digits to the left remain the same.

hundreds

4	5	7	3	2	5
4	5	7	3	0	0

up
(down)

---

16. Round to the indicated place value.

a) thousands

1	0	0	7	2	3
1	0	1	0	0	0

(up)
down

b) ten thousands

9	8	6	4	5	1

up
down

c) hundreds

3	1	7	2	2	6

up
down

d) hundred thousands

2	1	5	9	3	2	7

up
down

e) tens

3	8	5	7	2	0	6

up
down

f) hundred thousands

6	6	7	8	9	5	2

up
down

Sometimes in rounding you have to regroup.

Example: Round 37 952 to the nearest hundred.

3	7	9	5	2
		10		

Round 9 hundreds
up to 10 hundreds.

3	7	9	5	2
	8	0		

Regroup the 10 hundreds
as 1 thousand. Add it to the
7 thousands to make 8 thousands.

3	7	9	5	2
3	8	0	0	0

Complete the rounding.

BONUS ▶ Round the number, regrouping if necesary.

a) 395 721 to the ten thousands   b) 427 296 to the tens   c) 20 963 to the hundreds

NS6-6 Estimating in Addition and Subtraction

Mathematicians use the sign ≈ to mean **approximately equal to**.

1. Estimate the sums and differences by rounding to the nearest hundreds or thousands.

   a) 290 → | 300 |
       + 360 → + | 400 |
                 | 700 |

   b) 390 → | |
       + 460 → + | |
                 | |

   c) 6301 → | |
       − 1708 → − | |
                 | |

   d) 680 → | |
       + 160 → + | |
                 | |

   e) 470 → | |
       − 220 → − | |
                 | |

   f) 5610 → | |
       + 7240 → + | |
                 | |

   g) 941 − 463 ≈ _____

   h) 1267 + 5679 ≈ _____

   i) 5232 − 2854 ≈ _____

2. a) Estimate the difference in 1875 − 1532 by rounding to the nearest thousand. _____

   b) Estimate the difference in 1875 − 1532 by rounding to the nearest hundred. _____

   c) Which method makes more sense in the estimation? Explain. _____

   _____

   _____

   d) Circle the place value to which you will round each number when estimating the difference.

      i) 34 509 − 34 243   ii) 123 456 − 90 389   iii) 875 234 − 672 092   iv) 45 681 − 43 902

The **leading digit** is the leftmost digit of the number. The leading digit of 51 and 567 890 is 5.

3. Estimate. Then add or subtract. Hint: Which digit will you round to? It may not be the leading digit.

   a) 273 572 + 675 215 ≈ _____

   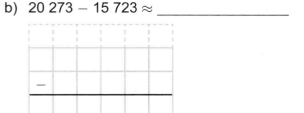

   b) 20 273 − 15 723 ≈ _____

   c) 80 278 − 42 325 ≈ _____

   d) 1 275 382 + 5 385 273 ≈ _____

   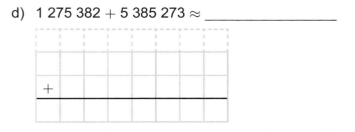

4. Follow the instructions to find the answer to the addition. Write the answer in the table below.

   a) Estimate the answer by rounding the numbers to the leading digit.

   b) Estimate the answer by rounding one number up and the other number down.
      Round to the leading digit.

   c) Estimate the answer by rounding both numbers up to the leading digit.

   d) Calculate the actual answer.

Part	3456 + 2391	32 901 + 44 789	372 987 + 573 004	64 870 + 28 705
a)	5000			
b)	6000			
c)	7000			
d)	5847			

   e) Circle the estimates from parts a), b), and c) that were closest to the actual answer in part d).

   f) Which way of estimating works best for addition? Explain. _____

   _____

   _____

5. Follow the instructions to find the answer to the subtraction. Write the answer in the table below.

   a) Estimate the answer by rounding the numbers to the leading digit.

   b) Estimate the answer by rounding one number up and the other number down.
      Round to the leading digit.

   c) Estimate the answer by rounding both numbers up to the leading digit.

   d) Calculate the actual answer.

Part	3456 − 2391	52 901 − 44 789	882 987 − 573 004	64 870 − 28 705
a)				
b)				
c)				
d)				

   e) Circle the estimates from parts a), b), and c) that were closest to the actual answer in part d).

   f) Which way of estimating works best for subtraction? Explain. _____

   _____

   _____

6. A supermarket sold 472 apples, 783 oranges, 341 pears, and 693 bananas. How many pieces of fruit in total did the supermarket sell? Use estimation to check your solution. Explain your estimation strategy.

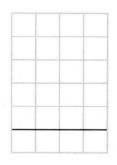

7. Round 628 315 to the nearest...

a) ten _____

b) hundred _____

c) thousand _____

d) ten thousand _____

e) hundred thousand _____

BONUS ▶ million _____

8. Luc is planning a trip from Sydney, NS, to Vancouver, BC. If he drives through Canada, the distance is 6032 km, which takes 63 hours to drive. If he drives through the United States, the distance is 6392 km, which takes 60 hours to drive. Luc plans to drive to Vancouver through Canada and return through the United States. What is the total distance Luc plans to drive? Estimate to check your answer.

9. An almanac lists the populations of Nova Scotia and PEI as 923 600 and 143 000. The numbers are rounded to the same digit. What digit are these numbers rounded to? Explain.

10. Rick calculated 45 780 + 23 451 = 89 231. Is Rick's answer correct? Use estimation to check.

11. Use the information in the table to answer the question. Then estimate to check your answer.

a) What is the total area of Manitoba and Saskatchewan?

b) How much larger is the area of Ontario than the area of British Columbia?

c) Make your own addition and subtraction questions using the information in the table. Calculate the answers.

Province	Area (km²)
Alberta	661 848
British Columbia	944 735
Manitoba	647 797
Ontario	1 076 395
Saskatchewan	651 036

NS6-7 Integers

The height above sea level and the depth below sea level are recorded on a scale that includes zero (0), **positive whole numbers** (1, 2, 3, …), and **negative whole numbers** (−1, −2, −3, …).

These numbers are called **integers**.

```
2  ┼  2 m above sea level
1  ┼  1 m above sea level
0  ┼  sea level
−1 ┼  1 m below sea level
−2 ┼  2 m below sea level
```

1. a) Write an integer for the level at which each animal typically flies or swims.

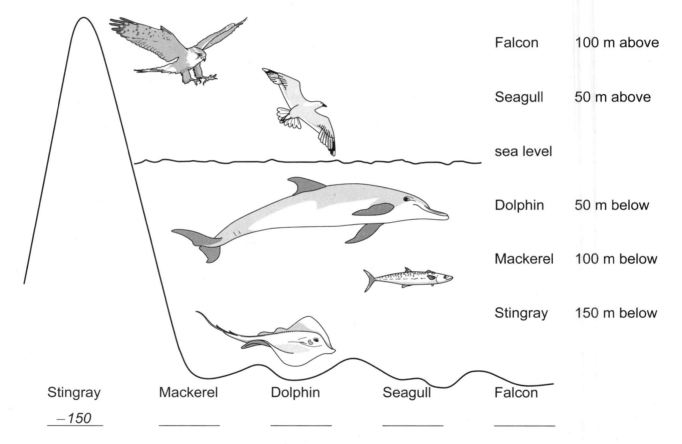

Falcon	100 m above
Seagull	50 m above
sea level	
Dolphin	50 m below
Mackerel	100 m below
Stingray	150 m below

Stingray	Mackerel	Dolphin	Seagull	Falcon
−150	_____	_____	_____	_____

b) Which animal swims above the other, the dolphin or the mackerel? _____

One integer is **greater than** another if it is

- higher up on a vertical number line or
- farther right on a horizontal number line.

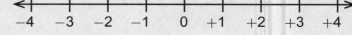

```
←──┼────┼────┼────┼────┼────┼────┼────┼────┼──→
  −4   −3   −2   −1    0   +1   +2   +3   +4
```

The inequality sign > means "is greater than" and < means "is less than."

c) Write an integer inequality to show your answer in part b): _____ < _____

Integers that are greater than 0 are called **positive integers**. Integers that are less than 0 are called **negative integers**.

Positive integers are sometimes written with a "+" sign in front. Example: 3 can be written as 3 or +3, but −3 is only written as −3.

2. Label the following numbers on the number line with their letters.

E. 6   **O.** − 3   **G.** −7   **L.** −5   **B.** 3

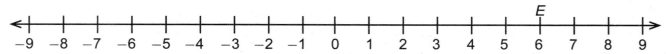

3. Write the integer on the number line.

a) −3   b) +3   c) −4   d) +7   e) −2   f) −5

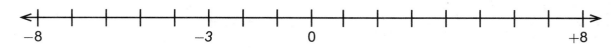

4. Circle the greater integer in the pair. Hint: Use the number line from Question 2.

a) −3 or +5   b) +7 or −2   c) +8 or +3   d) −5 or −4

5. a) Circle the integers on the number line: 3   −4   −8   −1   7

b) Order the integers you circled from least to greatest.

_____ < _____ < _____ < _____ < _____

6. Write < (is less than) or > (is greater than) in the box.

a) +3 ☐ +7   b) −5 ☐ +4   c) +7 ☐ −2   d) −4 ☐ −6

7. Put the integers into the boxes in order, from greatest to least.

+5, −3, +10, −7, −2   ⟶

8. Use any of the number lines above to answer the question.

a) How many negative integers are greater than (to the right of) −4? _____

b) What are 3 integers that are less than −5? _____, _____, _____

c) How many integers are between −4 and +2? _____

d) Which integers are closer together, −3 and +3 or −4 and +4? _____

Temperature is also recorded using integers. We use **degrees Celsius (°C)** to measure and record temperature.

9. Write "warmer" or "colder," then write > or < to show your answer.

   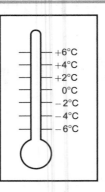

   a) +3°C is _____ than −4°C, so +3 ☐ −4.

   b) −5°C is _____ than −2°C, so −5 ☐ −2.

   c) −3°C is _____ than −6°C, so −3 ☐ −6.

10. The graph shows the average temperature on the planets in our solar system.

    a) What is the warmest average temperature?

       About _____ °C

    b) What is the coldest average temperature?

       About _____ °C

    BONUS ▶ What is the difference between the coldest average temperature and the warmest average temperature?

       About _____ °C

    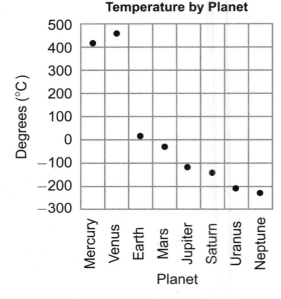

11. The temperature in Calgary, Alberta, was −8°C on Monday and −11°C on Tuesday.

    Which day was warmer? _____

Integers can be used to describe quantities having opposite directions from a given point.

Examples: temperatures above (+) and below (−) zero, golf scores above (+) and below (−) par, hours ahead of (+) or behind (−) London, UK.

12. Write an integer to represent the quantity.

    a) A temperature of fifty-two above zero _____

    b) A depth of two hundred meters below sea level _____

    c) A golf score of 5 shots above par _____

    d) A height of three hundred metres above sea level _____

    e) 5 hours behind London, UK _____

NS6-8 Opposite Integers

When two integers are the same distance from 0, but in opposite directions, they are called **opposite** integers. Example: +3 and −3 are opposite integers.

1. Use the number line above to write the opposite integer.

   a) +4 _____   b) −2 _____   c) +5 _____   d) −1 _____

The opposite of an integer has the same whole number part, but the opposite sign (+ or −).

Example: The opposite of −100 is +100.

2. The opposite of 429 is _____.

3. Circle the number that is closer to 0.

   a) −3 or −7   b) 3 or 7   c) −2 or +5   d) +2 or −5

4. Label each integer on the number line with its letter. What do the letters spell? _____

   N. the opposite of −6
   U. halfway between −1 and −5
   Y. on the same side of 0 as −3, but twice as far from 0 as −3

   O. halfway between +1 and +5
   K. an equal distance from +4 and −4

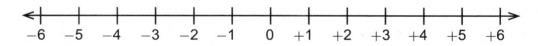

5. The integer 0 is halfway between…

   a) −2 and _____   b) −5 and _____   c) −12 and _____   d) −573 and _____

6. a) Use the number line to compare the positive numbers and their opposite negative numbers. Write < or >.

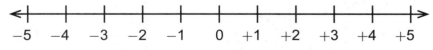

   i) 2 ☐ 5 and −2 ☐ −5   ii) 4 ☐ 3 and −4 ☐ −3

   iii) 3 ☐ 1 and −3 ☐ −1   iv) 2 ☐ 4 and −2 ☐ −4

   b) Predict using the pattern from part a): since 235 < 246, then −235 ☐ −246.

   BONUS ▶ What integer is equal to its opposite? Explain.

> **REMINDER ▶** Two integers are opposite integers if they are the same distance from 0 but in opposite directions.
>
> If you can compare positive integers, you can compare their opposite negative integers too.
>
> Example: 32 is **less than** 500, so −32 is **greater than** −500.

7. Compare the positive integers, then compare the negative integers.

a) +5421 $\boxed{<}$ +5432

    so −5421 $\boxed{>}$ −5432

b) +25 453 $\boxed{\phantom{<}}$ +23 674

    so −25 453 $\boxed{\phantom{<}}$ −23 674

c) +7000 $\boxed{\phantom{<}}$ +5982

    so −7000 $\boxed{\phantom{<}}$ −5982

d) 13 000 $\boxed{\phantom{<}}$ 14 000

    so −13 000 $\boxed{\phantom{<}}$ −14 000

e) 72 516 $\boxed{\phantom{<}}$ 75 216

    so −72 516 $\boxed{\phantom{<}}$ −75 216

f) +30 407 $\boxed{\phantom{<}}$ +3407

    so −30 407 $\boxed{\phantom{<}}$ −3407

8. Compare the negative integers by imagining their opposite positive integers.

a) −652 $\boxed{\phantom{<}}$ −1538

b) −809 417 $\boxed{\phantom{<}}$ −796 583

c) −6000 $\boxed{\phantom{<}}$ −40 000

9. Do you need to compare the numbers 38 and 27 to compare −38 to +27? _____

Explain. _____

_____

10. Write "greater than" or "less than" in the blank.

A negative integer is always _____ a positive integer.

11. Compare the integers. Write < or >.

a) −200 $\boxed{\phantom{<}}$ 100

b) 750 $\boxed{\phantom{<}}$ −4000

c) −800 $\boxed{\phantom{<}}$ −1000

d) −6000 $\boxed{\phantom{<}}$ 5000

e) 72 413 $\boxed{\phantom{<}}$ −5000

f) +853 416 $\boxed{\phantom{<}}$ +872 503

g) 751 602 $\boxed{\phantom{<}}$ 83 917

h) −615 893 $\boxed{\phantom{<}}$ −1 000 000

i) −983 417 $\boxed{\phantom{<}}$ 785 392

j) −62 953 $\boxed{\phantom{<}}$ 304 502

k) −621 419 $\boxed{\phantom{<}}$ +583 742

l) −8 217 354 $\boxed{\phantom{<}}$ −8 216 493

12. Use the digits 4, 5, 6, and 7 to create the number.

a) the greatest integer possible

b) the least integer possible

c) the greatest negative integer possible

d) a number between −6456 and −6576

PDM6-1 Bar Graphs and Double Bar Graphs

A **bar graph** has vertical and horizontal **axes**, a **scale**, a **title**, **labels**, and **data** (given by the bars).

The bars in a bar graph can either be **vertical** or **horizontal**. The scale helps to decide how tall the bars are. The labels indicate what the data in the bars is.

1. The table shows the number of pets owned by students in a Grade 6 class.

Pets Owned by Students	Number of Students
Cat	12
Dog	15
Reptile	6
Bird	3
Other	10

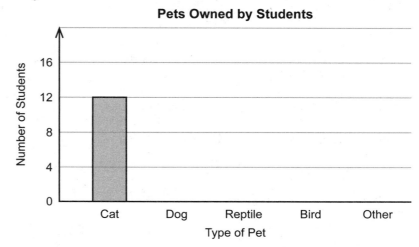

a) Complete the bar graph.

b) What do the axes show? Horizontal: _Type of Pet_ Vertical: _____

c) What number does the scale count by? _____ Do you think it was a good choice? Why or why not?

_____

2. a) Finish the bar graph to display the data. Use the letters B, M, I, Y, and T as short forms for the city names on your graph.

Temperatures by City (°C)	
Brandon, MB	25
Medicine Hat, AB	27
Iqaluit, NU	12
Yarmouth, NS	21
Thunder Bay, ON	24

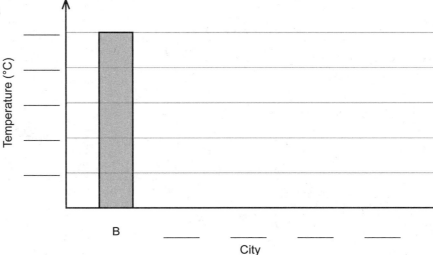

b) What number does the scale count by? _____

c) The **range** of a set of data is the difference between the largest and smallest values.

What is the range for this data? _____ – _____ = _____

3. The bar graphs show the votes in an election with two different scales.

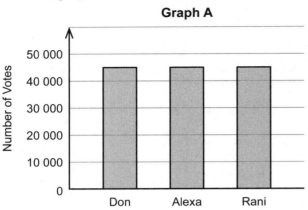

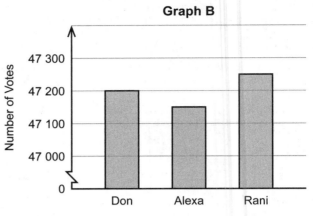

a) Describe the scale for Graph A: start at _____, count by _____, stop at _____.

b) Describe the scale for Graph B: start at _____, count by _____, stop at _____.

c) Which graph makes it easier to tell the difference in votes for each candidate? _____

d) Who won the election? _____

4. A roller skate company had $50 000 in sales in 2016, and $52 000 in sales in 2017.

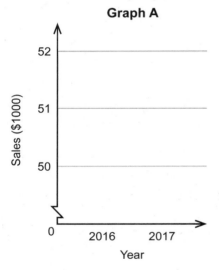

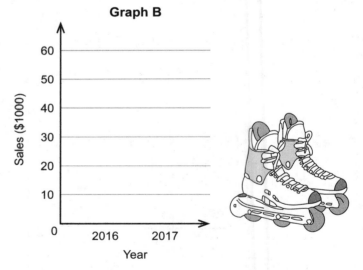

a) Show the data using the following two scales.

b) Which graph makes it appear as though the sales in 2017 were three times the sales in 2016? _____

c) Which graph makes it appear as though the sales in 2017 were only slightly greater than
    the sales in 2016? _____

d) Which graph do you think best represents the data? _____

5. What scale would you use if you had to plot the following numbers? (Say what numbers the
    scale would start and stop at, and what size the intervals would be). Explain your choices.

a) 3, 2, 7, 9, 10

b) 14, 2, 16, 4, 8

c) 250, 1000, 2000

d) 12 000, 11 500, 12 500

6. Two classrooms collected coats for charity from November to March.

Class A

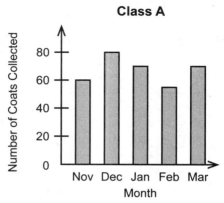

Class B

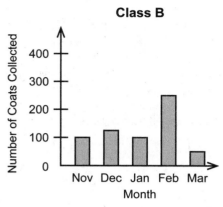

a) When you glance at the graphs, which class appears to have collected more coats? Explain.

_____

b) When you look closely at the scales, which class actually collected

more coats? _____

c) Why are most of Class B's data so low on the graph?

_____

_____

_____

_____

_____

d) To compare the data, complete the graph on the right.

Monthly Coat Collection for Two Classes

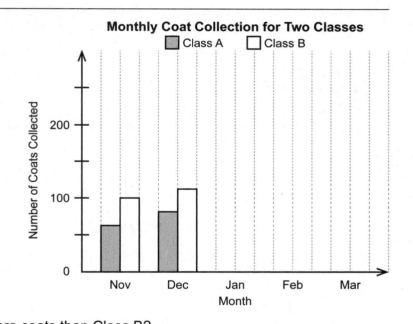

e) In which month(s) did Class A collect more coats than Class B? _____

f) During one month in this period, Class B put an ad in a newspaper asking for coats.

Which month do you think that was? _____

A **double bar graph** compares two sets of data. The graph you drew in Question 6 part d) is a double bar graph.

7. Draw a double bar graph using the data below. Include a title and labels.

Favourite Sports				
	Baseball	**Basketball**	**Tennis**	**Other**
Girls	42	32	73	56
Boys	75	50	43	80

PDM6-2 Stem and Leaf Plots

> The **leaf** of a number is its rightmost digit (ones digit).
>
> The **stem** is all its digits except the ones digit.
>
> The stem of a one-digit number is 0 since there are no digits except the rightmost one.

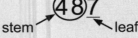

stem → 48⃝ 7̲ ← leaf

1. Circle the stem and underline the leaf.

   a) 5̲ *stem is 0*   b) ③7̲   c) 124   d) 51   e) 9000   f) 7

2. Circle the stems. Write the stems from smallest to largest.

   a) ②3 9 8 ③4 ⑥5 ②8 ②5   b) 36 39 46 51 37 9 45   c) 107 88 87 75 104 96

   _0_ _2_ _3_ _6_   ___ ___ ___ ___   ___ ___ ___ ___

> To build a stem and leaf plot for the data set 38 29 26 42 43 34:
>
> **Step 1:** Find the stems.   The stems are 3, 2, 4.
>
> **Step 2:** Write the stems from smallest to largest.   **Step 3:** Write the leaves for each stem in the leaf column.   **Step 4:** Order the leaves in each row from smallest to largest.
>
> | Stem | Leaf |
> |------|------|
> | 2 | |
> | 3 | |
> | 4 | |
>
> | Stem | Leaf |
> |------|------|
> | 2 | 9 6 |
> | 3 | 8 4 |
> | 4 | 2 3 |
>
> | Stem | Leaf |
> |------|------|
> | 2 | 6 9 |
> | 3 | 4 8 |
> | 4 | 2 3 |

3. Put the leaves in the correct order. Then list the data from smallest to largest.

   a)
Stem	Leaf
2	5 1 8 6
4	8 5 1
5	6 2 1

   →

Stem	Leaf
2	1 5
4	
5	

   _21_ , _25_ , ___ , ___ , ___ , ___ , ___ , ___ , ___ , ___

   b)
Stem	Leaf
0	7 4 1
1	9 3 6 5 2
2	5 8 0

   →

Stem	Leaf

   ___ , ___ , ___ , ___ , ___ , ___ , ___ , ___ , ___ , ___ , ___

4. Use the data to create a stem and leaf plot. (Remember to add a title.)

   a) Students' Ages: 8, 7, 11, 11, 10, 9, 6, 7, 10   b) Students' Marks: 89, 78, 97, 100, 88, 69, 75

PDM6-3 Continuous and Discrete Data, Broken Line Graphs

> Data is **continuous** if all numbers between data values are possible. Otherwise, the data is **discrete**.
> Non-numerical data is always discrete.

1. Is the data discrete or continuous?

   a) Shoe sizes: 5   5   6 $6\frac{1}{2}$ 7   7   7   8 $8\frac{1}{2}$

   Is size 6 1/4 possible? ___*No*___ The data is _____.

   b) Length of pencils (centimetres):   8   3   12   17.1   13.4   19   18.6

   Is length 8.5 cm possible? _____ The data is _____.

   c) Number of games won by contestants: 7   6   8   12   4   0   3

   Can a team win 6.5 games? _____ The data is _____.

   d) Distance Jen runs each day (in kilometres):   15   15   20   22   22   25

   Can there be half a _____? The data is _____.

   e) Number of runners Jen sees each day: 14   16   8   12   14

   Can there be half a _____? The data is _____.

2. Decide whether the data on each axis is discrete or continuous. Explain your answer.

   a)

   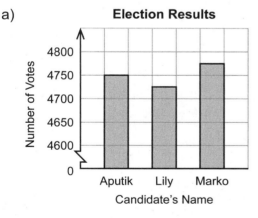

   Horizontal: _____

   _____

   _____

   Vertical: _____

   _____

   _____

   b)

   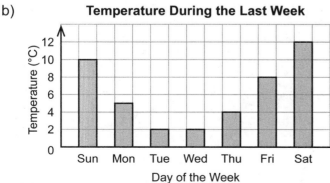

   Horizontal: _____

   _____

   _____

   Vertical: _____

   _____

   _____

In a **broken line graph**, individual points represent the data and are connected by line segments.

3. Look at the graph.

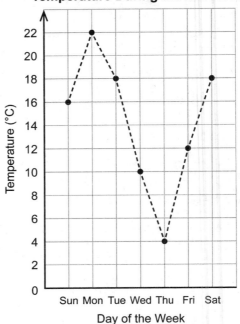

Temperature During the Last Week

a) Describe the scale. Start at _____,

count by _____, stop at _____.

b) What day was the coolest? _____

The warmest? _____

c) Which two days had the same temperature?

_____

d) What was the range of temperatures over

the week? _____ – _____ = _____

e) John says the temperature during the last week was above 12°C most of the time. Is John correct?

_____

4. The graph shows shoe sales over the past year.

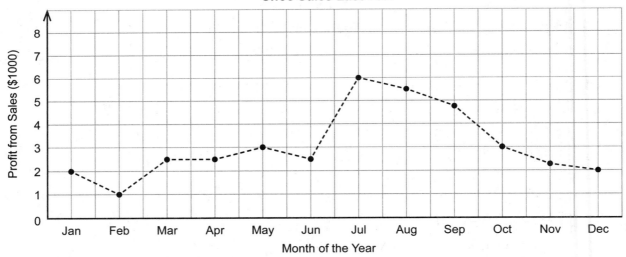

Shoe Sales Last Year

a) In which month did the shoe store make the largest profit? _____ The smallest profit? _____

b) Why might the smallest profit happen in a winter month? _____

c) In which months did the shoe store make more than $5000? _____

d) On which date do you think a star athlete signed shoes in the store?

February 1st   April 1st   July 1st   October 1st

Justify your answer: _____

PDM6-4 Reading and Predicting Graphs

You can use a ruler to find the exact height of a bar. You can also use a ruler on the graph on the right to see that 5 chapter books cost $25.

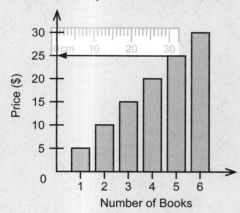 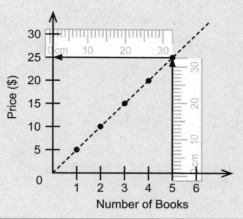

1. Use a ruler on the broken line graph above to find the cost.

   a) 3 books cost: $_____   b) 4 books cost: $_____   c) 6 books cost: $_____

2. To find out how many eBooks you can download for $12, start from the vertical axis and draw arrows as shown using a ruler. Find how many eBooks you can download.

   a) $3: _____ eBook

   b) $9: _____ eBooks

   c) $6: _____ eBooks

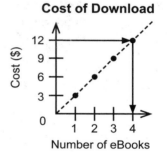

Cost of Download

3. These graphs show how much money Grace will earn painting houses in the summer.

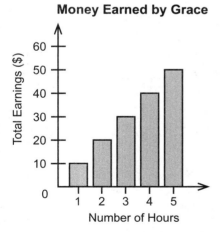 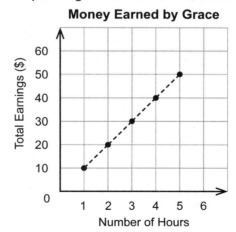

   a) On both graphs, show how much Grace would make for working: i) 3 hours   ii) 4 hours

   b) Extend the broken line graph to show how much Grace could make in 6 hours.

   c) Explain an advantage of a broken line graph over a bar graph.

   BONUS ▶ Draw arrows on the broken line graph to show how much Grace will earn in $3\frac{1}{2}$ hours.

A broken line graph is a good choice to display data if you want to predict what will happen outside the range of the data points.

4. As the temperature rises, crickets chirp more frequently.

   a) Extend the line to predict about how many times

   a cricket would chirp at 10°C. _____

   At 30°C? _____

   BONUS ▶ If a cricket chirps 90 times a minute, about how

   high would the temperature be? _____
   Explain how you found your answer.

   _____

   _____

   _____

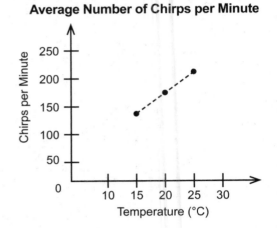

Average Number of Chirps per Minute

5. Emma wants to draw a graph of the data. She needs to answer a question using the data. Should she draw a broken line graph or a bar graph? Explain your choice.

   a) Will it be warmer or cooler next week?

Day	Sun	Mon	Tue	Wed	Thu	Fri	Sat
Temp (°C)	23	25	24	22	18	16	15

   _____

   b) Which city was warmest yesterday?

City	Toronto	Edmonton	Victoria	Winnipeg
Temp (°C)	27	24	19	25

   _____

   c) Will next year's profit be more or

   less than this year's? _____

Month	J	F	M	A	M	J	J	A	S	O	N	D
Profit ($1000)	3	2	3	3	4	4	5	5	5	6	6	7

   _____

BONUS ▶

   a) Did the company's earnings increase

   or decrease over time? _____

   b) What did the company do to make it
   look like their earnings increased
   over time?

   _____

   _____

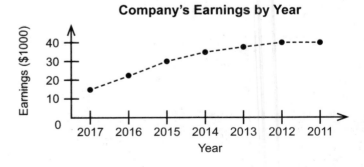

Company's Earnings by Year

PDM6-5 Continuous Line Graphs

A **continuous line graph** is similar to a broken line graph, but the lines are solid to show that the data is continuous on both axes. You can use a continuous line graph to predict what happens in between data values.

1. How far from home was Kathy after 10 minutes?

a)

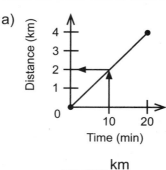

_____ km

b)

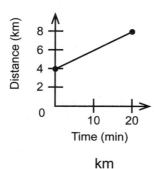

_____ km

c)

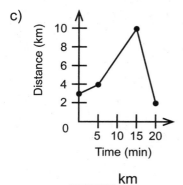

_____ km

2. Draw a continuous line graph, then answer the question.

a)

Time Worked (hr)	0	1	2	3	4
Money Earned ($)	0	10	20	30	40

How much money did Matt earn for $3\frac{1}{2}$ hours work?

_____

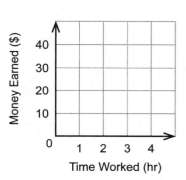

b)

Time (min)	0	1	2	3	4
Distance Walked (m)	0	100	200	300	400

How far did Lela walk in $2\frac{1}{2}$ minutes? _____

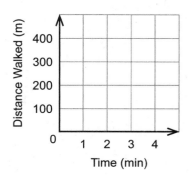

3. Sometimes graphs are drawn with solid lines (to show trends) even when data is not continuous.

a) Describe any trends you see in the graph.

b) Which data on the graph is not continuous? Explain.

c) Do you think the student would score over 90% by studying for more than one hour?

Do you feel confident about your prediction? Explain and discuss with your peers.

The Effect of Time Spent Studying

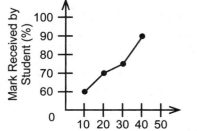

PDM6-6 Choosing and Interpreting Graphs

1. Cody wrote 12 math tests this year, each worth 100 marks. His marks were as follows:

Test #	1	2	3	4	5	6	7	8	9	10	11	12
Mark	68	73	75	82	78	75	78	78	83	86	93	91

a) Draw a stem and leaf plot and a broken line graph for Cody's math scores.

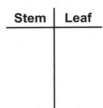

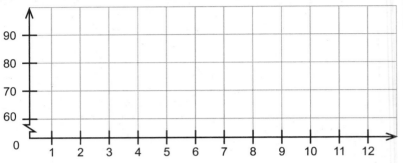

b) Answer the question and say which graph you used to find the answer.

i) On how many tests did he score between 78 and 88? _____

ii) What mark did he score most often? _____

iii) Did his marks tend to increase or decrease throughout the year? _____

iv) After which tests did his mark decrease? _____

v) What was his highest score? _____

2. The graph shows the number of concert tickets sold by classes in Avril's grade.

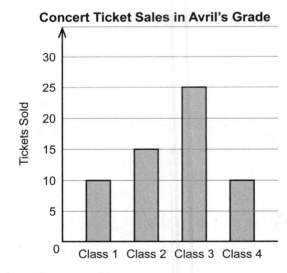

Concert Ticket Sales in Avril's Grade

a) How many tickets did Avril's grade sell altogether?

_____

b) Half of the tickets sold were adult tickets.

How many adult tickets were sold? _____

c) Adult tickets sell for $5.00 and student's tickets sell for $3.00. Calculate the total value of the tickets sold.

_____

_____

d) The money from the school concert is going toward a grade-wide excursion.

The bus for the event costs $300. How much more money is needed? _____

BONUS ▶ How many adult tickets would have to be sold to cover the remaining cost? How many student tickets?

_____

3. Choose and draw an appropriate type of graph to represent each set of data. Explain your choice.

a) Age and monthly allowance of different people.

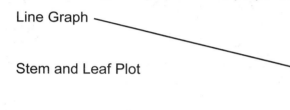

Age (year)	10	12	11	8	9	13
Monthly Allowance ($)	40	80	50	20	75	60

b) Thickness of rulers produced by a company (in tenths of a millimetre).

28   29   31   30   28   27   24   31   31   30   31   30   29   29   28   26   32   33   30   28

4. Match each type of graph with its purpose.

Line Graph   Compares two sets of data

Stem and Leaf Plot   Shows a trend in data or makes predictions

Double Bar Graph   Easy to see whether one type of data increases, decreases, or neither when comparing one type of data to the other

Bar Graph   Makes it easy to see the largest, smallest, and most common data values

5. The graph below displays the amount of money earned at a book sale over 7 days.

Book Sale Earnings

a) What is the range between the smallest and the largest amount of money earned over the 7 days? _____

b) From which day to which day is there the greatest increase in sales?

_____

c) How does the line graph show this?

_____

_____

6. a) Which graph best matches the data in each column? Write the letter of the correct graph under each column.

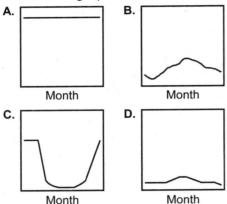

A. Month
B. Month
C. Month
D. Month

	Average Monthly Rainfall or Precipitation (mm)			
	Region A	Region B	Region C	Region D
January	25	10	100	120
February	20	10	100	120
March	25	10	100	120
April	35	10	20	120
May	45	13	10	120
June	50	18	5	120
July	60	18	5	120
August	55	13	5	120
September	50	10	10	120
October	40	10	20	120
November	40	10	50	120
December	35	5	100	120
Graph				

b) Describe any trends you see in the graphs. How do you account for each trend?

c) Sketch a graph that you think would represent the average monthly temperature where you live.

7. a) What is the size of the interval shown on the horizontal axis?

b) How many weeks does the interval represent?

c) Describe the trend you see in the graph.

d) The guinea pig was born at the beginning of January. In which month did it weigh 250 g?

e) During which months did it grow the fastest?

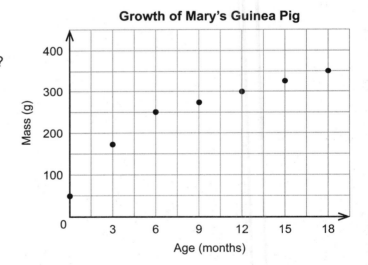

Growth of Mary's Guinea Pig

8. The table shows Canada's summer Olympic medal count from 1988 to 2016.

Year	1988	1992	1996	2000	2004	2008	2012	2016
Number of Summer Olympic Medals Won by Canada	10	18	22	14	12	20	18	22

a) State the range of the data.

b) Would you use a bar graph or a broken line graph to represent the data? Explain.

c) Graph the data.

To multiply 2 × 30, Cam makes 2 groups of 3 tens blocks (30 = 3 tens).

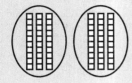

To multiply 2 × 300, Cam makes 2 groups of 3 hundreds blocks (300 = 3 hundreds).

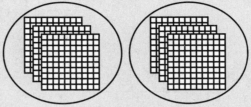

2 × 30 = 2 × 3 tens = 6 tens = 60

2 × 300 = 2 × 3 hundreds = 6 hundreds = 600

Cam notices a pattern: 2 × 3 = 6   2 × 30 = 60   2 × 300 = 600

1. Draw a model for the multiplication. Then calculate the answer.

   a) 2 × 40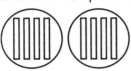

   b) 3 × 30

   2 × 40 = 2 × _____ tens = _____ tens = _____   3 × 30 = 3 × _____ tens = _____ tens = _____

2. Regroup to find the answer.

   a) 3 × 70 = 3 × __7__ tens = __21__ tens = __210__

   b) 4 × 60 = 4 × _____ tens = _____ tens = _____

   c) 5 × 70 = 5 × _____ tens = _____ tens = _____

   d) 8 × 40 = 8 × _____ tens = _____ tens = _____

3. Complete the pattern.

   a) 3 × 2 = _____   b) 7 × 1 = _____   c) 2 × 4 = _____   d) 7 × 2 = _____

   3 × 20 = _____   7 × 10 = _____   2 × 40 = _____   7 × 20 = _____

   3 × 200 = _____   7 × 100 = _____   2 × 400 = _____   7 × 200 = _____

4. Multiply.

   a) 4 × 20 = _____   b) 3 × 30 = _____   c) 2 × 40 = _____   d) 3 × 50 = _____

   e) 7 × 100 = _____   f) 2 × 300 = _____   g) 3 × 400 = _____   h) 6 × 200 = _____

   i) 5 × 70 = _____   j) 4 × 60 = _____   k) 9 × 20 = _____   l) 8 × 300 = _____

5. Draw a base ten model to show 3 × 2000. Use a cube to represent a thousand.

6. You know that 4 × 2 = 8. How can you use this fact to multiply 4 × 2000?

$10 \times \square =$ ▯

10×1 one $= 1$ ten

$10 \times$ ▯ $= \square$

10×1 ten $= 1$ hundred

$10 \times \square =$ (cube)

10×1 hundred $= 1$ thousand

7. Draw a model for the multiplication. Then calculate the answer.

a) $10 \times 20 = 10 \times$ ▯▯ $= \square\square$ $= \underline{\quad 200 \quad}$

b) $10 \times 300 = 10 \times \square\square\square = $ (cubes) $= \underline{\quad\quad}$

c) $10 \times 30 = 10 \times$ ▯▯▯ $=$ $= \underline{\quad\quad}$

d) $10 \times 4 = \underline{\quad\quad}$

e) $10 \times 40 = \underline{\quad\quad}$

f) $10 \times 400 = \underline{\quad\quad}$

8. Multiply.

a) $10 \times 5 = \underline{\quad\quad}$

b) $10 \times 60 = \underline{\quad\quad}$

c) $10 \times 30 = \underline{\quad\quad}$

d) $10 \times 200 = \underline{\quad\quad}$

e) $10 \times 8 = \underline{\quad\quad}$

f) $10 \times 400 = \underline{\quad\quad}$

BONUS ▶

g) $10 \times 30\ 000\ 000 = \underline{\quad\quad}$

h) $50\ 000 \times 10 = \underline{\quad\quad}$

$10 \times 12 = 120$	$100 \times 12 = 1200$	$1000 \times 12 = 12\ 000$

9. Use the pattern in the grey box to multiply.

a) $10 \times 17 = \underline{\quad\quad}$

b) $100 \times 17 = \underline{\quad\quad}$

c) $10 \times 24 = \underline{\quad\quad}$

d) $1000 \times 43 = \underline{\quad\quad}$

e) $100 \times 78 = \underline{\quad\quad}$

f) $1000 \times 32 = \underline{\quad\quad}$

BONUS ▶

g) $1000 \times 253 = \underline{\quad\quad}$

h) $34 \times 1000 = \underline{\quad\quad}$

To multiply 20 × 60, Tessa multiplies (2 × 10) × (6 × 10).

A 20 × 60 rectangle can be divided into 12 rectangles
of 10 × 10 each. Tessa multiplies:

$20 \times 60 = (2 \times 10) \times (6 \times 10)$

$\qquad = (2 \times 6) \times (10 \times 10)$

$\qquad = 12 \times 100$

$\qquad = 1200$ ◄——— 12 rectangles of 10 × 10

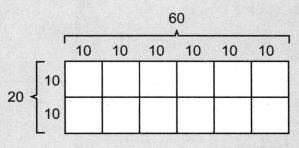

10. Multiply.

a) $30 \times 40 = (3 \times 10) \times (4 \times 10)$

$\qquad = (3 \times 4) \times (10 \times 10)$

$\qquad = 12 \times \underline{\quad 100 \quad}$

$\qquad = \underline{\quad 1200 \quad}$

b) $20 \times 70 = (2 \times 10) \times (7 \times 10)$

$\qquad = (2 \times 7) \times (10 \times 10)$

$\qquad = \underline{\qquad} \times \underline{\qquad}$

$\qquad = \underline{\qquad}$

c) $20 \times 400 = (2 \times 10) \times (4 \times 100)$

$\qquad = (2 \times 4) \times (10 \times 100)$

$\qquad = 8 \times \underline{\quad 1000 \quad}$

$\qquad = \underline{\quad 8000 \quad}$

d) $40 \times 400 = (4 \times 10) \times (4 \times 100)$

$\qquad = (4 \times 4) \times (10 \times 100)$

$\qquad = \underline{\qquad} \times \underline{\qquad}$

$\qquad = \underline{\qquad}$

Follow the steps to multiply 40 × 700:

Step 1: Multiply 4 × 7 = 28.

Step 2: Write all the zeros from **40** and **700**. ——► 40 × 700 = 28 **000**

11. Multiply the one-digit numbers to find the product of the tens and hundreds.

a) $8 \times 4 = \underline{\quad 32 \quad}$

$80 \times 400 = \underline{\quad 32\ 000 \quad}$

b) $4 \times 3 = \underline{\qquad}$

$40 \times 300 = \underline{\qquad}$

c) $5 \times 9 = \underline{\qquad}$

$50 \times 900 = \underline{\qquad}$

d) $2 \times 6 = \underline{\qquad}$

$20 \times 600 = \underline{\qquad}$

e) $4 \times 7 = \underline{\qquad}$

$40 \times 700 = \underline{\qquad}$

f) $8 \times 5 = \underline{\qquad}$

$80 \times 500 = \underline{\qquad}$

BONUS ▶ Estimate 3128 × 4956 by rounding each number first. 3000 × 5000 = \underline{\qquad}

12. Multiply.

a) $30 \times 200 = \underline{\qquad}$

b) $400 \times 20 = \underline{\qquad}$

c) $70 \times 300 = \underline{\qquad}$

NS6-10 Dividing Using Tens

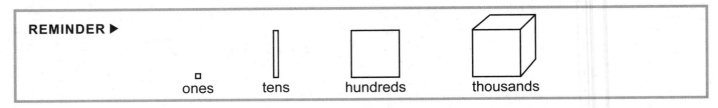

REMINDER ▶

ones   tens   hundreds   thousands

1. Divide the blocks into two equal groups. Then write the division equation.

   a) 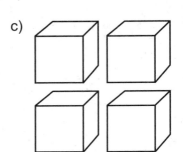 ___6___ ÷ 2 = ___3___

   b) ___60___ ÷ 2 = _____

   c) _____ ÷ 2 = _____

   d) _____ ÷ 2 = _____

2. Divide into equal groups. Then finish the division equation.

   a) 8 tens ÷ 4 = ___2___ tens   so 80 ÷ 4 = ___20___

   b) 12 hundreds ÷ 3 = _____ hundreds   so 1200 ÷ 3 = _____

   c) 6 thousands ÷ 2 = _____ thousands so 6000 ÷ 2 = _____

   d) 32 thousands ÷ 8 = _____ thousands so 32 000 ÷ 8 = _____

3. Divide.

   a) 9 ÷ 3 = _____   b) 20 ÷ 4 = _____

       90 ÷ 3 = _____   200 ÷ 4 = _____

       900 ÷ 3 = _____   2000 ÷ 4 = _____

       9000 ÷ 3 = _____   20 000 ÷ 4 = _____

4. Divide.

   a) 800 ÷ 2 = _____   b) 600 ÷ 3 = _____   c) 12 000 ÷ 4 = _____

   d) 14 000 ÷ 7 = _____ e) 25 000 ÷ 5 = _____ f) 24 000 ÷ 6 = _____

5. Write a division statement for each part of the picture. Then complete the equation.

a)

<u>   15 ÷ 3   </u>

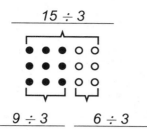

<u> 9 ÷ 3 </u>   <u> 6 ÷ 3 </u>

<u> 15 ÷ 3 = (9 ÷ 3) + (6 ÷ 3) </u>

b)

<u>   </u>

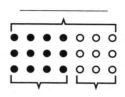

<u>   </u>   <u>   </u>

<u>   </u>

c)

<u>   </u>

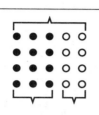

<u>   </u>   <u>   </u>

<u>   </u>

d)

<u>   </u>

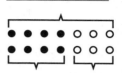

<u>   </u>   <u>   </u>

<u>   </u>

6. Write an equivalent division statement. Then find the answer.

a) $46 = 40 + 6$

so $46 ÷ 2 =$ <u> $(40 ÷ 2) + (6 ÷ 2)$ </u>

$=$ <u> $20 + 3$ </u>

$=$ <u> 23 </u>

b) $69 = 60 + 9$

so $69 ÷ 3 =$ <u>   </u>

$=$ <u>   </u>

$=$ <u>   </u>

c) $75 = 60 + 15$

so $75 ÷ 3 =$

d) $120 = 100 + 20$

so $120 ÷ 2 =$

e) $72 = 60 + 12$

so $72 ÷ 3 =$

f) $96 = 80 + 16$

so $96 ÷ 4 =$

7. Find the answer using a pair of easier division statements.

a) $165 ÷ 3 =$ <u> $(150 ÷ 3) + (15 ÷ 3)$ </u>

$=$ <u> $50 + 5$ </u>

$=$ <u> 55 </u>

b) $318 ÷ 3 =$ <u>   </u>

$=$ <u>   </u>

$=$ <u>   </u>

c) $172 ÷ 2$

d) $81 ÷ 3$

e) $94 ÷ 2$

f) $292 ÷ 4$

8. Divide mentally. Explain how you found the answer to parts e) and h).

a) $63 ÷ 3$

b) $65 ÷ 5$

c) $84 ÷ 7$

d) $78 ÷ 6$

e) $600 ÷ 30$

f) $1260 ÷ 60$

g) $31\ 500 ÷ 50$

h) $427 ÷ 7$

NS6-11 Mental Math

This is how Alexa multiplies **4 × 22**:

She rewrites 22 as a sum: 22 = 20 + 2

She multiplies 4 by 20:   4 × 20 = 80

She multiplies 4 by 2:   4 × 2 = 8

She adds the two results: 80 + 8 = 88

Alexa concludes that **4 × 22 = 88**.

This picture shows why Alexa's method works:

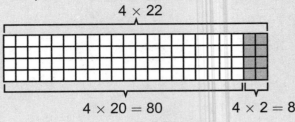

$$4 \times 22 = (4 \times 20) + (4 \times 2) = 80 + 8 = 88$$

---

1. Use the picture to write the multiplication as a sum.

a)

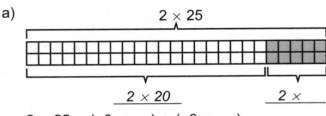

2 × 25 = (_2 ×_) + (_2 ×_)

b)

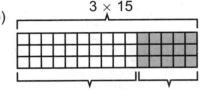

3 × 15 = (_____) + (_____)

2. Multiply using Alexa's method.

a) 5 × 13 = ___5 × 10___ + ___5 × 3___ = ___50 + 15___ = _____65_____

b) 4 × 21 = _____ + _____ = _____ = _____

c) 3 × 43 = _____ + _____ = _____ = _____

d) 2 × 432 = ___2 × 400___ + ___2 × 30___ + ___2 × 2___ = ___800 + 60 + 4___ = ___864___

e) 3 × 312 = _____ + _____ + _____ = _____ = _____

f) 4 × 321 = _____ + _____ + _____ = _____ = _____

3. Multiply in your head by multiplying the digits separately.

a) 3 × 12 = _____   b) 3 × 52 = _____   c) 6 × 31 = _____   d) 7 × 21 = _____

e) 5 × 31 = _____   f) 3 × 42 = _____   g) 6 × 51 = _____   h) 2 × 44 = _____

i) 4 × 521 = _____   j) 3 × 621 = _____   k) 5 × 411 = _____   l) 2 × 444 = _____

m) 3 × 632 = _____   n) 4 × 422 = _____   o) 4 × 212 = _____   p) 2 × 421 = _____

4. a) Jen placed 821 books in each of 4 bookshelves.
   How many books did she place altogether?

   b) David put 723 pencils in each of 3 boxes.
   How many pencils did he put in the boxes?

5. Double the number mentally by doubling the ones digit and the tens digit separately.

a) double 24 is ___48___   b) double 14 is _____   c) double 12 is _____

d) double 13 is _____   e) double 51 is _____   f) double 43 is _____

g) double 71 is _____   h) double 84 is _____   i) double 93 is _____

6. Double the ones and tens separately and add the result.

a) double 16 is _20 + 12 = 32_   b) double 26 is _____   c) double 37 is _____

d) double 46 is _____   e) double 48 is _____   f) double 19 is _____

g) double 54 is _____   h) double 78 is _____   i) double 89 is _____

Anton doubles 23 twice to find 23 × 4:

Double 23 is 46, and double 46 is 80 + 12 = 92. So 23 × 4 is 92.

---

7. Double twice to find the answer.

a) 31 × 4

Double 31 is ___62___,

and double _62_ is _120 + 4 = 124_.

So 31 × 4 is _124_.

b) 17 × 4

Double 17 is _____,

and double _____ is _____.

So 17 × 4 is _____.

c) 73 × 4

Double 73 is _____,

and double _____ is _____.

So 73 × 4 is _____.

d) 48 × 4

Double 48 is _____,

and double _____ is _____.

So 48 × 4 is _____.

Mandy puts pairs that make a multiple of 10 together to find the product mentally:

$5 \times 13 \times 2 = 5 \times 2 \times 13 = 10 \times 13 = 130$ $4 \times 16 \times 5 = 4 \times 5 \times 16 = 20 \times 16 = 320$

---

8. Multiply by finding a multiple of 10.

a) $5 \times 31 \times 4 =$ ___5 × 4 × 31___

= ___20 × 31___ = ___620___

b) $2 \times 39 \times 5 =$ _____

= _____ = _____

c) $6 \times 22 \times 5 =$ _____

= _____ = _____

BONUS ▶ 8 × 12 × 5

NS6-12 The Standard Method for Multiplication

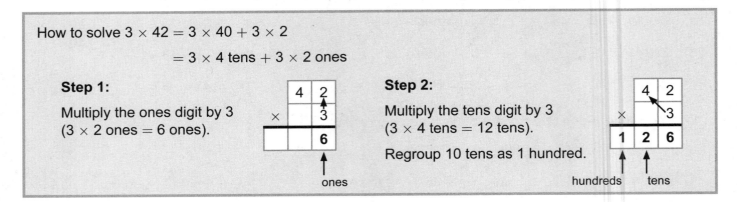

How to solve $3 \times 42 = 3 \times 40 + 3 \times 2$

$= 3 \times 4$ tens $+ 3 \times 2$ ones

Step 1:

Multiply the ones digit by 3
(3×2 ones $= 6$ ones).

Step 2:

Multiply the tens digit by 3
(3×4 tens $= 12$ tens).

Regroup 10 tens as 1 hundred.

1. Multiply.

a)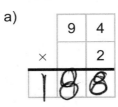
b)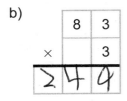
c)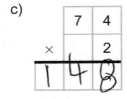
d)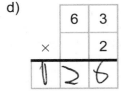
e)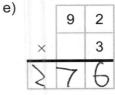

How to solve $7 \times 53 = 7 \times 50 + 7 \times 3$

$= 7 \times 5$ tens $+ 7 \times 3$ ones

Step 1:

Multiply 3 ones by 7
($7 \times 3 = 21$).

Step 2:

Regroup 20 ones as 2 tens.

2. Multiply the ones digits and regroup.

a)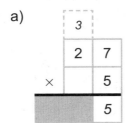
b)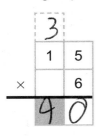
c)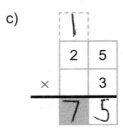
d)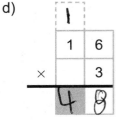
e)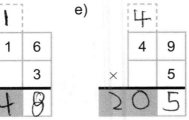

f)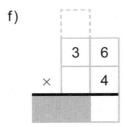
g)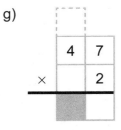
h)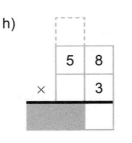
i)
j)

Step 3:		Step 4:	
Multiply 5 tens by 7 (7 × 5 tens = 35 tens).	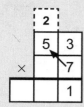	Add 2 tens to the result (35 + 2 = 37 tens).	

3. Complete the multiplication using **Steps 3** and **4**.

a)
```
    1
   2 4
 ×   3
 ─────
   7 2
```

b)
```
    4
   3 5
 ×   9
 ─────
     5
```

c)
```
    2
   1 5
 ×   5
 ─────
     5
```

d)
```
    1
   7 3
 ×   5
 ─────
     5
```

e)
```
    4
   8 9
 ×   5
 ─────
     5
```

4. Complete **all steps** of the multiplication.

a)
```
   3 5
 ×   9
 ─────
```

b)
```
   3 5
 ×   6
 ─────
```

c)
```
   1 5
 ×   7
 ─────
```

d)
```
   2 5
 ×   8
 ─────
```

e)
```
   2 4
 ×   5
 ─────
```

5. Multiply. Regroup ones as tens.

a)
```
   2 2 7
 ×     3
 ───────
```

b)
```
   1 1 6
 ×     5
 ───────
```

c)
```
   2 2 4
 ×     3
 ───────
```

d)
```
   1 1 9
 ×     5
 ───────
```

e)
```
   3 2 8
 ×     3
 ───────
```

6. Multiply. Regroup when you need to.

a)
```
    1 3
   2 3 7
 ×     5
 ───────
   1 0 5 5
```

b)
```
    0 0 1
   4 3 2 5
 ×       3
 ─────────
   1 2 9 7 5
```

c)
```
    0 1 0
   1 3 2 5 4
 ×         2
 ───────────
   1 6 5 0 8
```

7. A dog is 13 years old. Multiply that by 7 to estimate the dog's age in human years.

8. Anna borrowed a library book for 21 days. She reads 9 pages each day. If the book is 165 pages long, will she need to renew the book?

NS6-13 Multiplication (2-Digit by 2-Digit)

To multiply 37 × 20, first multiply 37 × 2, then multiply by 10.
This is how to record your answer on a grid:

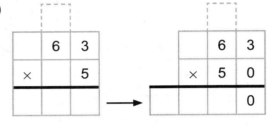 × 10 →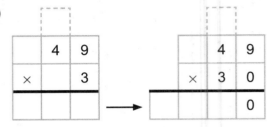

1. Multiply.

a) 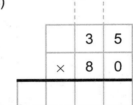 →

b) 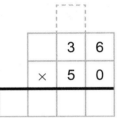 →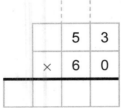

c)

d)

e)

f)

To multiply 37 × 25, split 25 into two numbers that are easier to multiply by. The picture shows why this works.

a multiple of 10 ↘   a one-digit number ↙

$37 \times 25 = 37 \times \mathbf{20} + 37 \times \mathbf{5}$

$\quad\quad\quad = 740 + 185$

$\quad\quad\quad = 925$

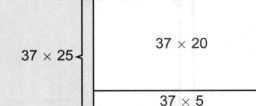

37×25

2. Multiply. Do the rough work in your notebook.

a) 34 × 27

$34 \times 20 =$ _____

$34 \times 7 =$ _____

so $34 \times 27 =$ _____

b) 56 × 32

$56 \times 30 =$ _____

$56 \times 2 =$ _____

so $56 \times 32 =$ _____

c) 83 × 26

$83 \times 20 =$ _____

$83 \times 6 =$ _____

so $83 \times 26 =$ _____

d) 78 × 45

$78 \times 40 =$ _____

$78 \times 5 =$ _____

so $78 \times 45 =$ _____

You can record the steps in multiplying two-digit numbers on a grid. Example: Find 37×25.

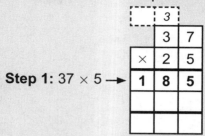

Step 1: 37×5 →

		3	
		3	7
×		2	5
	1	**8**	**5**

Step 2: 37×20 →

	1	3	
		3	7
×		2	5
	1	8	5
	7	**4**	**0**

Step 3: Add results →

	1	3	
		3	7
×		2	5
	1	8	5
	7	4	0
	9	**2**	**5**

3. Practise Step 1.

a)

	1	
	2	4
×	1	3
	7	2	$= 24 \times 3$

b)

	3	3
×	3	9

c)

	5	2
×	4	4

d)

	1	6
×	3	5

4. Practise Step 2.

a)

	1	
	3	4
×	4	3
1	0	2	$= 34 \times 40$

b)

	1	
	6	9
×	5	2
1	3	8

c)

	1	
	5	2
×	3	6
3	1	2

d)

	3	
	6	7
×	2	5
3	3	5

5. Practise Steps 1 and 2.

a) Regrouping for 35×20 → Regrouping for 35×6 →

		3	5
	×	2	6
				$= 35 \times 6$
			0	$= 35 \times 20$

b)

		3	2
	×	5	4

c)

		4	5
	×	3	5

d)

		1	6
	×	4	2

6. Multiply.

a)

		3	7
	×	2	5
+			0

b)

		6	9
	×	5	3
+			0

c)

		7	4
	×	5	2

d)

		5	4
	×	3	2

Multiplying 354 × 48 can be broken up into steps:

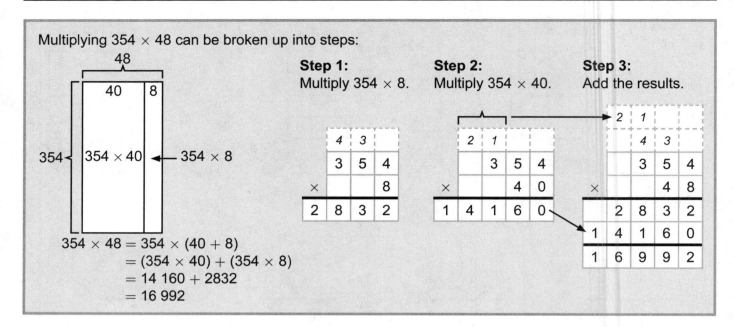

Step 1:
Multiply 354 × 8.

Step 2:
Multiply 354 × 40.

Step 3:
Add the results.

$$354 \times 48 = 354 \times (40 + 8)$$
$$= (354 \times 40) + (354 \times 8)$$
$$= 14\,160 + 2832$$
$$= 16\,992$$

1. Multiply, showing the three steps.

a) 756 × 52

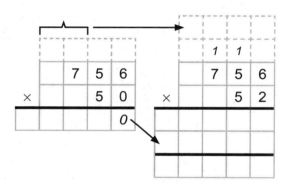

b) 328 × 46

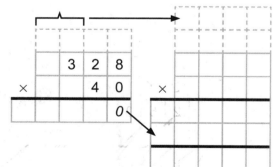

c) 572 × 29

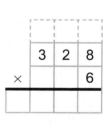
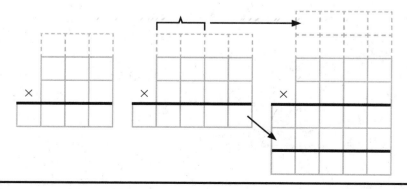

Matt multiplies 463 × 58. He uses a grid to keep track of the steps of multiplication:

Step 1: He multiplies 463 × 8.

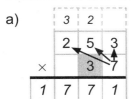

$8 \times 3 = 24$

$(8 \times 6) + 2 = 50$

$(8 \times 4) + 5 = 37$

2. Practise the first step of multiplication.

a)
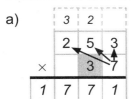

b)
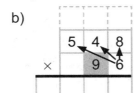

c)
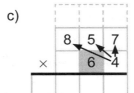

d)
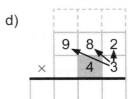

Step 2: Matt continues multiplying 463 × 58 by multiplying 463 × 50. To avoid confusion with the regrouping, he crosses out the regrouping done in the first step.

$5 \times 3 = 15$

$(5 \times 6) + 1 = 31$

$(5 \times 4) + 3 = 23$

— Cross out the regrouping done in Step 1.

— Don't forget the zero!

3. Practise the second step of multiplication.

a)
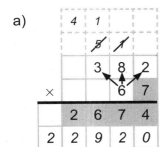

b)
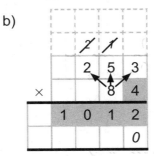

c)
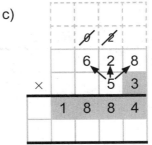

d)
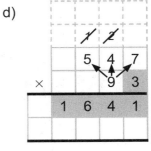

e)
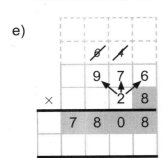

f)
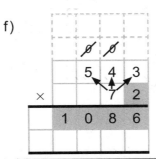

g)
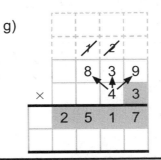

h)
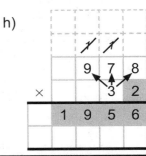

4. Practise Steps 1 and 2 of multiplication.

a)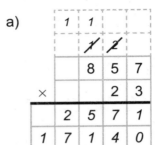

b)

		6	8	9
×			4	2
				0

c)

		3	2	9
×			5	7

d)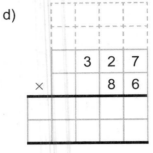

e)

		9	2	8
×			5	4

f)

		5	2	3
×			9	1

g)

		8	0	4
×			5	6

h)

		9	1	6
×			7	5

Step 3: Matt completes the multiplication by adding the products of 463 × 50 and 463 × 8.

5. Multiply.

a)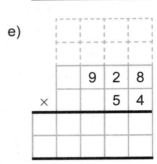

b)

		5	1	4
×			7	8

c)

		3	0	7
×			9	5

d)

		3	6	5
×			2	4

e)

	3	2	4	5
×			7	3

BONUS ▶

f)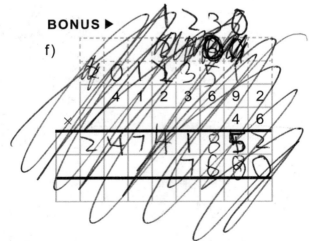

g)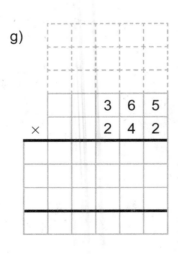

		3	6	5
×			2	4	2

NS6-15 Multiplication Word Problems

1. There are 1760 yards in one mile. How many yards are in eight miles?

2. A household in Nova Scotia spends $248 on heating fuel each month. How much does the household spend on heating in six months?

3. A local school is buying televisions to put in their Grade 6 classrooms. The televisions cost $439 each. How much will the school pay to buy a television for each of their six Grade 6 classes?

4. Tom is working during the summer to help pay for hockey and his equipment. He earns $450 per week. How much will he earn in eight weeks of summer?

5. A school is selling raffle tickets to raise money. The average student sells $9 worth of tickets. There are 523 students in the school. How much money is raised?

6. There were 1 989 705 households in the GTA (Greater Toronto Area) in 2011. If there are three people in each household, what was the population of the GTA in 2011?

7. The word "level" is a palindrome because the letters can be read forward or backward for the same result. Show that the number 412 107 multiplied by 3 is a palindrome.

8. A farmer's field has the shape of a pentagon. Each of its five sides is 921 metres long.

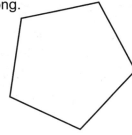

   a) What is the perimeter of the field in metres?

   b) The farmer has 4500 metres of wire fence. How many more metres of fence will the farmer need to surround the field?

9. Lela spends $7 each weekday on lunch.

   a) How many weekdays are in a year?

   b) How much money does she spend on lunch in a year?

   c) Lela only budgeted $1720 for lunch. How far over her budget was she?

10. A baseball stadium holds 32 459 fans. The average fan spent $8 on a ticket.

   a) How much money was collected from ticket sales?

   b) If the stadium could hold 33 000 fans, how much money could be collected from ticket sales?

11. Sharon spends 24 hours on her tablet each week. How many hours does she use her tablet in one year?

12. Jack pays $47 per month in cell phone fees. How much does he pay each year in cell phone fees?

13. Tristan buys an electric car and makes payments of $449 each month. How much will Tristan pay for his car in the first year?

14. Megan is a professional basketball player. She earns $1617 per game. She plays 34 games in one year. How much does Megan earn in one year?

15. The Wilson family bought farmland. The land is in the shape of a rectangle with a length of 273 m and a width of 98 m. What is the area of the land in square metres (m^2)?

16. A minute has 60 seconds. Each hour has 60 minutes.

a) How many seconds are in an hour?

b) There are 24 hours in one day. How many seconds are in one day?

c) There are 7 days in a week. How many seconds are in one week?

BONUS ▶ There are 365 days in a year. How many minutes are in one year?

17. In some countries, it costs only $18 to buy lunch for a child for an entire year.

a) How much money is needed to pay for lunch for a school of 354 children for the entire year?

b) A generous donor gave $5000 to the school. How much more money is needed to feed all the children for one year?

18. Jayden needs 130 megabytes of storage space for each album he downloads to his smartphone. Jayden has 54 albums stored on his phone. His phone can store 7930 megabytes of songs. How many more megabytes of songs can he store?

19. The speed of sound is about 343 metres per second. How many metres does sound travel in 1 hour?

NS6-16 Long Division

Divide 334 objects into 2 groups using long division and a base ten model:

Step 1: Divide the hundreds into 2 groups.

```
    1
2) 3 3 4
  -2
   1
```
← 1 hundred in each group
← 2 hundreds placed
← 1 hundred left over

Step 2: Regroup the remaining hundreds as tens.

```
    1
2) 3 3 4
  -2↓
   1 3
```
← 13 tens

1. Do the first two steps of long division.

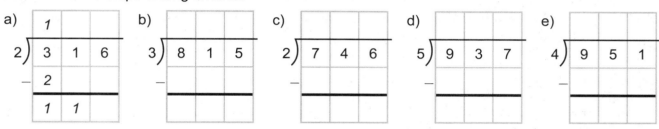

a)
```
    1
2) 3 1 6
  -2
   1 1
```

b)
```
3) 8 1 5
  -
```

c)
```
2) 7 4 6
  -
```

d)
```
5) 9 3 7
  -
```

e)
```
4) 9 5 1
  -
```

Step 3: Divide the tens into 2 groups.

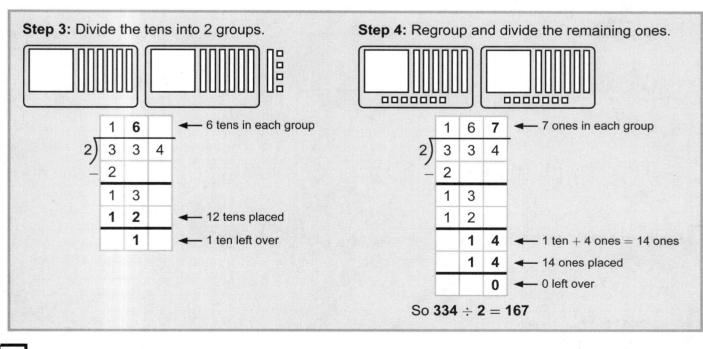

```
    1 6
2) 3 3 4
  -2
   1 3
   1 2
     1
```
← 6 tens in each group

← 12 tens placed
← 1 ten left over

Step 4: Regroup and divide the remaining ones.

```
    1 6 7
2) 3 3 4
  -2
   1 3
   1 2
     1 4
     1 4
       0
```
← 7 ones in each group

← 1 ten + 4 ones = 14 ones
← 14 ones placed
← 0 left over

So **334 ÷ 2 = 167**

2. Divide. Use grid paper.

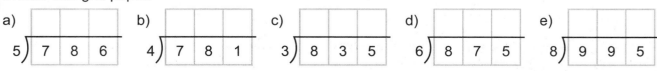

a)
```
5) 7 8 6
```

b)
```
4) 7 8 1
```

c)
```
3) 8 3 5
```

d)
```
6) 8 7 5
```

e)
```
8) 9 9 5
```

3. Here there are fewer hundreds than the number of groups. Write "0" in the hundreds place to show that no hundreds can be placed in equal groups. Then perform the division as if the hundreds had been exchanged for tens.

a)
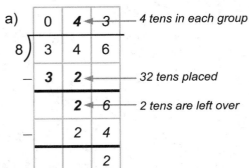
```
    0   4   3  ← 4 tens in each group
8 ) 3   4   6
  - 3   2     ← 32 tens placed
        2   6 ← 2 tens are left over
      - 2   4
            2
```

b)
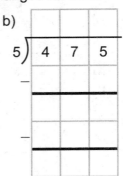
```
5 ) 4   7   5
```

c)
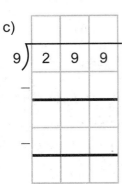
```
9 ) 2   9   9
```

d)
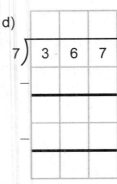
```
7 ) 3   6   7
```

e) 3)115   f) 4)341   g) 8)425   h) 6)379   i) 9)658

4. Here there are not enough tens to divide into the groups. Write "0" in the tens place to show that no tens can be placed, then continue the division, regrouping tens as ones.

a)
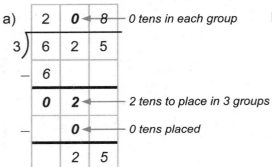
```
    2   0   8  ← 0 tens in each group
3 ) 6   2   5
  - 6
    0   2      ← 2 tens to place in 3 groups
  - 0          ← 0 tens placed
        2   5
      - 2   4
            1
```

b)
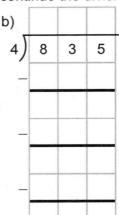
```
4 ) 8   3   5
```

c)
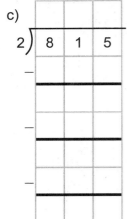
```
2 ) 8   1   5
```

d)
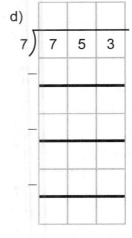
```
7 ) 7   5   3
```

5. Divide.

a) 3)417   b) 4)821   c) 8)725   d) 6)9731   e) 5)23 731

6. Fruit juice bottles cost $3. How many bottles can be purchased with $142?

7. A car can hold five people. How many cars will 1387 passengers need?

8. A store has enough golf balls to sell eight customers 36 golf balls each. If there are nine customers, how many golf balls could each customer buy?

NS6-17 Estimating

1. Round to the nearest ten.

a) 22 _20_   b) 26 _____   c) 73 _____   d) 58 _____

e) 94 _____   f) 89 _____   g) 40 _____   h) 35 _____

2. Round to the nearest hundred.

a) 362 _400_   b) 641 _____   c) 470 _____   d) 941 _____

e) 703 _____   f) 800 _____   g) 750 _____   h) 349 _____

> **REMINDER ▶** The **leading digit** is the digit on the left of a number.
> Examples: The leading digit of 41 is 4, and the leading digit of 7293 is 7.

3. Round to the leading digit.

a) 873 _900_   b) 1730 _2000_   c) 68 _____   d) 747 _____

e) 2342 _____   f) 50 _____   g) 4700 _____   h) 38 _____

> ≈ ◀— Mathematicians use this symbol to mean "approximately equal to."

4. Estimate the product by rounding to the nearest hundred.

a) $123 \times 281 \approx$ _100 × 300 = 30 000_   b) $542 \times 181 \approx$ _____

c) $209 \times 483 \approx$ _____   d) $768 \times 821 \approx$ _____

5. Estimate the product by rounding to the leading digit.

a) $33 \times 175 \approx$ _30 × 200 = 6000_   b) $492 \times 81 \approx$ _____

c) $307 \times 12 \approx$ _____   d) $2759 \times 812 \approx$ _____

e) $42 \times 511 \approx$ _____   f) $62 \times 3921 \approx$ _____

6. Is the product reasonable? Explain why.

a) $417 \times 205 = 75\ 485$ _____

b) $293 \times 411 = 120\ 423$ _____

c) $194 \times 286 = 61\ 484$ _____

7. Divide by multiples of 10.

a) $600 \div 30 =$ _60 ÷ 3 = 20_   b) $800 \div 20 =$ _____

c) $1200 \div 40 =$ _____   d) $3600 \div 90 =$ _____

8. Estimate the quotient by rounding to the leading digit.

   a) $213 \div 52 \approx$ _____*200 ÷ 50 = 4*_____

   b) $397 \div 82 \approx$ _____

   c) $507 \div 11 \approx$ _____

   d) $5835 \div 279 \approx$ _____

   e) $903 \div 29 \approx$ _____

   f) $7941 \div 394 \approx$ _____

9. Predict the range where the product or quotient will be.

   A. 1 to 10   **B.** 11 to 100   **C.** 101 to 500   **D.** 501 to 1000   **E.** above 1000

   a) 31×27 _D_

   b) $4279 \div 70$ ____

   c) $13\,200 \div 600$ ____

   d) 45×87 ____

   e) $4521 \div 91$ ____

   f) 3×23 ____

   g) $742 \div 83$ ____

   h) 11×42 ____

   Use a calculator to check your prediction.

10. Shelly multiplied a one-digit number by a three-digit number. The product was about 1000. Write three very different pairs of numbers she might have multiplied.

11. A wedding party dinner costs $34 per guest. Estimate the dinner cost for 220 guests.

   BONUS ▶ Do you think this is a good estimation? Why?

12. Table tennis balls come in packs of 6 for $5.97. Each table tennis racket is $39.98. Dory has $100. Does Dory have enough money to buy 3 packs of balls and 2 rackets?

ME6-1 Estimating and Measuring Length

1. Estimate the length in centimetres. Then measure the length to the closest centimetre.

	Object	Estimate	Actual Length
a)	pencil case		
b)	eraser		
c)	book		
d)	you choose:		

---

1 centimetre = 10 **millimetres**   1 cm = 10 **mm**

---

2. a) Fill in the measurements in millimetres.

cm	1	2	3	4	5	6	7	8
mm	*10*							

b) To change a measurement from centimetres (cm) to millimetres (mm), what number

do you multiply by? _____

3. Convert the measurement in centimetres to millimetres.

a) 9 cm = _____ mm   b) 12 cm = _____ mm   c) 15 cm = _____ mm

d) 34 cm = _____ mm   e) 152 cm = _____ mm   f) 1675 cm = _____ mm

---

Amy wants to find a mark for 23 mm on a ruler.

She counts millimetre marks from 2 cm = 20 mm to 23 mm.

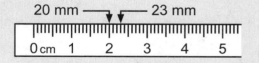

---

4. Find the length in millimetres.

a)
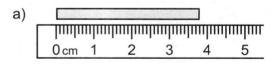

_____ mm

b)

_____ mm

c)
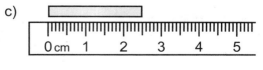

_____ mm

d)
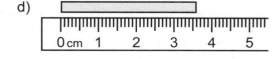

_____ mm

Measurement 6-1   **75**

5. Estimate the length in millimetres. Then measure the length in millimetres.

	Object	Estimate	Actual Length
a)	pencil		
b)	sharpener		
c)	your partner's hand		
d)	you choose:		

---

1 metre = 100 centimetres   1 m = 100 cm

---

6. a) Fill in the measurements in centimetres.

m	1	2	3	4	5	6	7	8
cm	100							

   b) To change a measurement from metres (m) to centimetres (cm), what number

   do you multiply by? _____

7. Convert the measurement in metres to centimetres.

   a) 9 m = _____ cm   b) 11 m = _____ cm   c) 45 m = _____ cm

   d) 60 m = _____ cm   e) 173 m = _____ cm   f) 6670 m = _____ cm

8. a) Estimate the length of your classroom in metres. _____

   b) Measure the length of your classroom to the closest metre. _____

---

1 **decimetre** = 10 cm   1 **dm** = 10 cm   1 m = 10 dm

1 **decametre** = 10 m   1 **dam** = 10 m

---

9. Fill in the table.

dam	1	2	3	4	5	6
m	10	20				
dm	100					
cm	1000					
mm	10 000					

10. Convert the measurements and fill in the table.

a)
m	cm
7	
25	
136	

b)
m	dm
9	
44	
850	

c)
dam	m
8	
30	
407	

d)
cm	mm
10	
69	
130	

e)
m	mm
9	
46	
702	

f)
dm	cm
7	
34	
500	

11. Convert the measurement in larger units to smaller units. Circle the shorter measurement.

a) 573 cm   7 m

b) 989 mm   9 m

c) 78 dm   799 cm

d) 6 dam   63 m

e) 678 cm   6782 mm

f) 78 dm   8 m

12. Convert the part in metres to centimetres. Add the leftover centimetres.

a) 5 m 3 cm

= _____500_____ cm + __3__ cm

= _____503_____ cm

b) 4 m 68 cm

= _____ cm + _____ cm

= _____ cm

c) 10 m 30 cm

= _____ cm + _____ cm

= _____ cm

d) 9 m 17 cm

= _____ cm + _____ cm

= _____ cm

e) 18 m 5 cm

= _____ cm + _____ cm

= _____ cm

f) 105 m 3 cm

= _____ cm + _____ cm

= _____ cm

13. a) Convert all the measurements to the same unit.

Bird	Wingspan	Wingspan	Rank
Bald eagle	2 m 30 cm		
Brown pelican	1 m 97 cm		
Calliope hummingbird	110 mm		
Northern cardinal	3 dm		
Ring-billed gull	112 cm		

b) Rank the birds by wingspan from longest (1) to shortest (5).

ME6-2 Metres and Kilometres

We measure large distances in **kilometres** (km). 1 kilometre = 1000 metres

1. a) How many hundreds are there in 1000? _____

    b) A football field is about 100 m long. How many football fields long is 1 km? _____

2. You can walk 1 km in about 15 minutes. Name a place that is about 1 km from your school.

_____

3. a) Fill in the table.

km	1	2	3	4	5	6	7	8
m	1000							

    b) To change a measurement from kilometres to metres, what number do you

    multiply by? _____

4. Convert the measurement in kilometers to meters. Then circle the greater measurement.

    a) 500 m   ⬭7 km⬭   b) 5300 m   61 km   c) 35 678 m 8 km

                 7000 m

    d) 2345 m   2 km   e) 70 km   7200 m   f) 72 km   45 203 m

5. a) Write a measurement in metres that is between 6 km and 7 km. _____

    b) Write a measurement in kilometres that is between 3250 m and 4728 m. _____

6. What unit would you use to measure the distance: metres (m) or kilometres (km)?

    a) From your home to the school _____   b) From your classroom to the cafeteria _____

    c) Around the schoolyard _____   d) Between Ottawa and Sudbury, ON _____

    Explain one of your answers.

_____

_____

_____

7. The number line represents 1 km. Mark the distance on the number line.

a) 200 m   b) 50 m   c) 550 m   d) 825 m   e) 110 m   f) 999 m

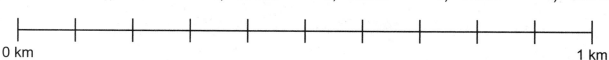

0 km   1 km

8. A speed skating track is 400 m long.

a) Kate skates twice around the track. How many metres does she skate? _____

b) Kate skates 5 times around the track. How many kilometres does she skate? _____

c) About how many times must Kate skate around the track to cover 3 km? _____

   How do you know? _____

   _____

9. Convert the part in kilometres to metres. Add the leftover metres.

a) 2 km 3 m

   = ___2000___ m + ___3___ m

   = ___2003___ m

b) 4 km 168 m

   = _____ m + _____ m

   = _____ m

c) 1 km 30 m

   = _____ m + _____ m

   = _____ m

d) 3 km 250 m

   = _____ m + _____ m

   = _____ m

e) 10 km 4 m

   = _____ m + _____ m

   = _____ m

f) 70 km 25 m

   = _____ m + _____ m

   = _____ m

10. The table lists the heights of some mountains in Canada.

a) Change the heights to metres.   b) Rank the mountains from highest (1) to lowest (4).

Mountain	Height	Height (m)	Rank
Mount Columbia	3 km 747 m		
Mount Fairweather	4671 m		
Mount Logan	5959 m		
Mount Vancouver	4 km 812 m		

11. Horse race distances are measured in furlongs. There are 8 furlongs in 1 mile. 1 mile is about 1 km 609 m.

a) The Breeders' Stakes race is 12 furlongs long. About how many metres long is the race?

b) The Queen's Plate race is 10 furlongs long. The Prince of Wales's Stakes race is 1910 m long. Which race is longer? How much longer?

ME6-3 Selecting Units

> A dime is about 1 mm thick.
>
> Your hand is about 1 dm wide.
>
> A school bus is about 1 dam long.
>
> Your finger is about 1 cm wide.
>
> A giant step is about 1 m long.
>
> 10 football fields are about 1 km long.

1. Draw a line to match the object to the best unit to measure it.

   a) length of a small spider   dam   b) height of a person   km

       length of a city block   mm   distance to Antarctica   cm

   c) height of a chair   m   d) width of a door   km

       height of a tree   km   width of the St. Lawrence River   dm

       height of a mountain   cm   width of a pencil   mm

   e) length of a feather   mm   f) height of a building   km

       length of a long street   cm   width of Lake Ontario   cm

       width of a street   dam   length of a small lizard   m

       thickness of a cell phone   km   thickness of a coin   mm

2. Circle the measurement that best fills the blank.

   a) A piece of cardboard is about _____ thick.   5 mm   5 cm   5 dm   5 m

   b) To plant a bush, dig a hole _____ deep.   50 cm   50 m   50 dam   50 km

   c) A blueberry bush is about _____ tall.   15 mm   15 dm   15 m   15 km

   d) It is about _____ from Kitchener, ON, to Timmins, ON.   800 cm   800 dm   800 m   800 km

   e) A firetruck ladder is _____ long.   3 dm   3 m   3 dam   3 km

   f) A human eye measures _____ across.   24 mm   24 cm   24 dm   24 m

   g) A small car is about _____ long.   3 cm   3 dm   3 m   3 dam

3. Eric says that these two houses must be the same height, because they are both 1 dam tall. Measuring in which unit would help Eric avoid this mistake? Explain.

   _____

   _____

   _____

1 dam

REMINDER ▶ 1 cm = 10 mm	1 dm = 10 cm	1 m = 10 dm = 100 cm

4. A flower bed is 120 cm long.

    a) How many decimetres long is the flower bed? _____ dm

    b) How many metres long, to the closest metre, is the flower bed? _____ m

    c) How many millimetres long is the flower bed? _____ mm

    d) Which unit (m, dm, cm, or mm) gives the simplest measurement? _____

5. A button is 2 mm thick.

    a) Write the thickness to the closest unit.

    i) _____ cm   ii) _____ dm    iii) _____ m

    b) Which unit gives the most information about the thickness of the button? Explain.

    _____

    _____

    c) Rick is making holes for the buttons. If the hole is too small, the button will not fit.
    If the hole is too large, the button will slip out of the hole all the time.

    Does Rick need to know the precise width and thickness of the buttons in millimetres,
    or is an estimate enough? Explain.

    _____

    _____

    _____

6. Marla wants to decorate the sides of a gift box she made with ribbon.
She does not want the ribbon to overlap.

    a) Measure the sides of the gift box to the closest centimetre.
    Add the side lengths.

    _____ cm + _____ cm + _____ cm + _____ cm = _____ cm

    b) Measure the sides of the gift box in millimetres. Add the side lengths.

    _____ mm + _____ mm + _____ mm + _____ mm = _____ mm

    c) Did you get the same total length of ribbon? _____

    d) Which answer should Marla use to cut the ribbon? _____

    Which unit is better for Marla's problem? _____

7. Vicky wants to know about how much time it will take to drive from her home to a party.

   a) Which unit is best to measure the distance? _____

   b) Does Vicky need to know the exact distance or is an estimate enough? Explain.

   _____

   _____

8. Josh's ceiling is 2 m 40 cm tall. A bookshelf is about 18 dm tall.

   a) Will the bookshelf fit inside the room? _____

   b) Does Josh need to know the exact height of the bookshelf to know if it will fit, or is the estimate enough? Explain.

   _____

   _____

   c) Josh wants to add an extension that is about 6 dm tall on top of the bookshelf. Does he need to know the exact height of the shelf and the extension, or is the estimate enough? Explain.

   _____

   _____

9. Kim's room is 3 m 75 cm long.

   a) How many metres long (to the closest metre) is Kim's room? _____

   b) How many centimetres long is Kim's room? _____

   c) Write the measurements in the table in centimetres and in metres to the closest metre.

Object	Length	Length in cm	Length in m
bed	19 dm		
shelf	85 cm		
desk	1 m 23 cm		

   d) Add the lengths of the objects in part c) in metres. Do you think the objects will fit along the length of Kim's room? Explain.

   _____

   _____

   e) Is an estimate in metres enough to see if the objects will fit along the length of Kim's room, or do you need the precise measurements? Explain.

ME6-4 Perimeter

The distance around the outside of a shape is called the **perimeter** of the shape. The perimeter of this figure, made from 1 cm squares, is 6 cm.

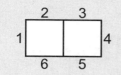

1. Each square side is 1 cm long. Find the perimeter in centimetres.

a)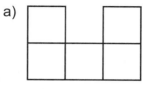

_____ cm

b)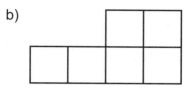

_____ cm

c)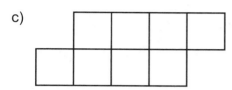

_____ cm

2. Find the perimeter of the garden by writing an addition statement.

a)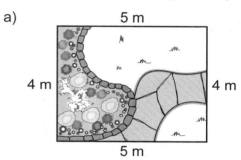

Perimeter = _____

b)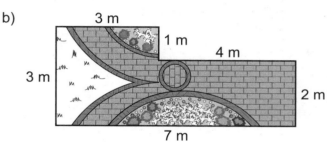

Perimeter = _____

3. Each square is 1 cm long. Write the total length of each side beside the figure.
   Then write an addition statement to find the perimeter.

a)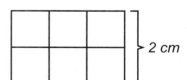

Perimeter = _____

b)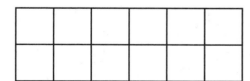

Perimeter = _____

c)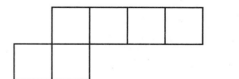

Perimeter = _____

d)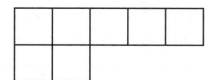

Perimeter = _____

4. Each square on the grid is 3 cm long. Write the length of each side beside the figure. Then add the side lengths to find the perimeter.

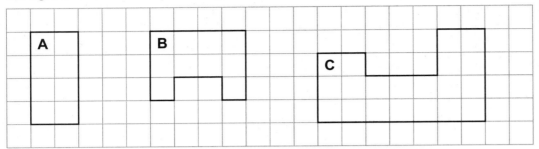

Perimeter **A** = _____

Perimeter **B** = _____

Perimeter **C** = _____

_____

_____

_____

> **REMINDER ▶** 1 m = 100 cm   2 m = 2 × 100 = 200 cm

5. Convert the side lengths to centimetres. Then find the perimeter. Include the units in your answer.

a)
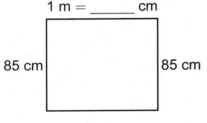

1 m = _____ cm

85 cm   85 cm

1 m = _____ cm

Perimeter = _____

b)
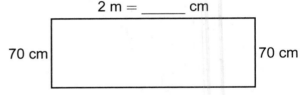

2 m = _____ cm

70 cm   70 cm

2 m = _____ cm

Perimeter = _____

c)
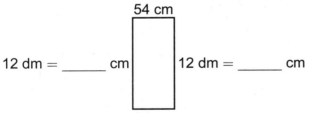

54 cm

12 dm = _____ cm   12 dm = _____ cm

54 cm

Perimeter = _____

d)
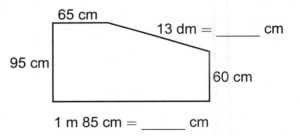

65 cm   13 dm = _____ cm

95 cm   60 cm

1 m 85 cm = _____ cm

Perimeter = _____

6. a) Rob thinks the perimeter of the rectangle shown is 164 cm. Sandy thinks the perimeter of the rectangle is 164 m. Are they correct? Explain.

   b) Convert the side lengths to centimetres and find the perimeter.

   c) Convert the side lengths to decimetres and find the perimeter.

   d) Compare your answers in parts b) and c). Did you get the same perimeter? If not, find your mistake.

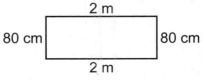

2 m

80 cm   80 cm

2 m

Measurement 6-4

7. Each square is 1 unit long. Write the perimeter of each figure in the sequence.

_____   _____   _____   _____

   a) How does the perimeter change each time a square is added?

   _____

   b) What would the perimeter of the 6th figure be? _____

8. Each hexagon has sides of 4 m. Write the perimeter of each figure in the sequence.

_____   _____   _____   _____

   a) How does the perimeter change each time a hexagon is added?

   _____

   b) What would the perimeter of the 6th figure be? _____

9. a) Perimeter: _____

   Add one square so that the perimeter of the figure increases by 2.

   New perimeter: _____

   b) Perimeter: _____

   Add one square so that the perimeter of the figure stays the same.

   New perimeter: _____

10. Draw your own figure and find its perimeter. Draw the sides of the figure along the grid lines only.

ME6-5 Perimeter Formulas

1. Find the missing side lengths of the rectangle. Then add the side lengths to find the perimeter P.

a)

5 m, 3 m, 3 m, 5 m

$P = \underline{3\,m + 5\,m + 3\,m + 5\,m}$

$ = \underline{16\,m}$

b)

4 m, 2 m

$P = \underline{\hphantom{xxxxxxxxxxx}}$

$ = \underline{\hphantom{xxxxx}}$

c)

6 m, 8 m

$P = \underline{\hphantom{xxxxxxxxxxx}}$

$ = \underline{\hphantom{xxxxx}}$

2. Find the missing side lengths of the rectangle. Then use multiplication and addition to find the perimeter.

a)

4 cm, 3 cm, 3 cm, 4 cm

$P = \underline{(2 \times 3\,cm) + (2 \times 4\,cm)}$

$ = \underline{6\,cm + 8\,cm}$

$ = \underline{14\,cm}$

b)

4 dm, 1 dm

$P = \underline{\hphantom{xxxxxxxxxxx}}$

$ = \underline{\hphantom{xxxxx}}$

$ = \underline{\hphantom{xxx}}$

c)

6 km, 5 km

$P = \underline{\hphantom{xxxxxxxxxxx}}$

$ = \underline{\hphantom{xxxxx}}$

$ = \underline{\hphantom{xxx}}$

d)

10 mm, 4 mm

$P = \underline{\hphantom{xxxxxxxxxxx}}$

$ = \underline{\hphantom{xxxxx}}$

$ = \underline{\hphantom{xxx}}$

e)

3 dam, 1 dam

$P = \underline{\hphantom{xxxxxxxxxxx}}$

$ = \underline{\hphantom{xxxxx}}$

$ = \underline{\hphantom{xxx}}$

f)

L, W

$P = \underline{\hphantom{xxxxxxxxxxx}}$

$ = \underline{\hphantom{xxxxx}}$

$ = \underline{\hphantom{xxx}}$

3. Use the formula for the perimeter of the rectangle you found in Question 2, part f) to find the perimeter of the rectangle.

a) Length = 100 m

Width = 50 m

b) Length = 1000 m

Width = 800 m

c) Length = 30 000 cm

Width = 25 000 cm

BONUS ▶ Length = 4321 km, Width = 1234 km

A rectangle has perimeter 14 m. Each side is a whole number of metres.

What are the dimensions of the rectangle? Try different widths. Start with 1 m.

The widths add to 2 m.
The missing lengths are 14 m − 2 m = 12 m altogether.
Each length is 12 m ÷ 2 = 6 m.

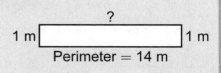

Perimeter = 14 m

4. a) The widths add to _____ m.

   b) The missing lengths are 14 m − _____ m = _____ m altogether.

   c) Each missing length is _____ m ÷ 2 = _____ m.

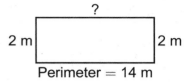

Perimeter = 14 m

5. a) The widths add to _____ m.

   b) The missing lengths are _____ altogether.

   c) Each missing length is _____ m.

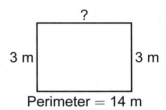

Perimeter = 14 m

6. Find the missing measurements.

   a) Perimeter = 18 m

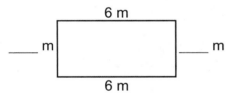

   b) Perimeter = 10 cm

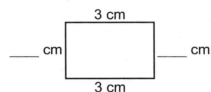

   c) Perimeter = 24 cm

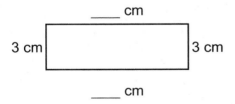

   d) Perimeter = 16 m

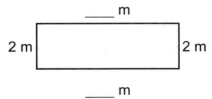

7. Use grid paper to draw all possible rectangles with the given perimeter. Start with width 1 unit, then try 2 units, and so on.

   a) 14 units   b) 6 units   c) 8 units   d) 10 units

   BONUS ▶ Find all possible rectangles with the given perimeter (with widths and lengths that are whole numbers). Use a table to stay organized.

   a) Perimeter = 6 m   b) Perimeter = 12 dm

   c) Perimeter = 16 cm   d) Perimeter = 18 km

8. a) A square has sides 5 cm long. What is its perimeter?

  b) How could you find the perimeter of a square without drawing a picture?

  c) A square has a perimeter of 12 cm. How long is one side? Explain.

  d) A square has a perimeter of 1 m. How long is each side? Explain.

9. Find the missing side lengths of the square. Then use multiplication to find the perimeter.

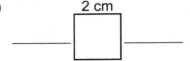 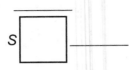

  a) _____   b)   2 cm   c) _____

  _____ 6 m   _____ [ ] _____   S[ ] _____

  _____   _____   _____

  $P =$ _____ $P =$ _____ $P =$ _____

  $=$ _____ $=$ _____ $=$ _____

10. Use the formula for the perimeter of the square you found in Question 9, part c) to find the perimeter of the square.

  a) Side length = 100 m   b) Side length = 40 m   c) Side length = 3000 cm

11. Circle the quantities that can change in the formula. Underline the quantities that do not change.

  a) $P = 4S$ b) $P = 2L + 2W$

12. Sally arranged five paper squares (each with 1 m sides) to make a poster. She wants to make a border from ribbon for her poster.

  Ribbon costs 60¢ for each metre. How much will the border cost?   1 m {⬜⬜⬜⬜⬜

13. Can two different rectangles have the same perimeter? Use grid paper to explain.

14. Emma says the rule "2 × (length + width)" gives the perimeter of a rectangle. Is she correct?

15. A rectangular room is 3 m 28 cm long and 1 m 95 cm wide. It has one doorway that is 95 cm wide. Jay needs to install quarter round around the perimeter of the room, not including the doorway.

  a) How much quarter round is needed?

  b) Quarter round is sold in rods of 2 m 40 cm. How many rods should Jay buy?

  c) Quarter round costs $5 per rod. How much will Jay pay for the quarter round?

ME6-6 Mass

Mass is the amount of matter in an object. The heavier an object, the greater its mass.
The mass of small objects is often measured in **grams** (g).

A large paper clip weighs about 1 gram.

1. The mass of a nickel is about 4 g.

   a) What is the mass of 10 nickels? _____ 50 nickels? _____

   b) What is the mass of the amount in nickels?

   i) 5¢ _____   ii) 50¢ _____   iii) 80¢ _____   iv) 100¢ _____

2. Estimate the mass of the object in grams. Measure the mass to the nearest gram.

   a) pencil case   b) banana

      Estimate: _____ Measure: _____   Estimate: _____ Measure: _____

   c) shoe   d) you choose: _____

      Estimate: _____ Measure: _____   Estimate: _____ Measure: _____

Mass is also measured in **kilograms** (kg).

A tall thin carton of orange juice has a mass of 1 kg.

1 kilogram = 1000 grams   1 kg = 1000 g

---

3. Estimate and circle the correct mass for the item.

   a)   b)   c)    d)

      2 g or 2 kg   15 g or 15 kg   35 g or 35 kg   270 g or 270 kg

4. Estimate the mass of the object in kilograms. Measure the mass to the nearest kilogram.

   a) backpack   b) heavy book

      Estimate: _____ Measure: _____   Estimate: _____ Measure: _____

   c) large bottle of water   d) you choose: _____

      Estimate: _____ Measure: _____   Estimate: _____ Measure: _____

5. How many whole kilograms are in the measurement?

   a) 3648 g _3 kg_   b) 6723 g _____   c) 20 000 g _____   d) 879 g _____

6. a) Fill in the table.

kg	1	2	3	4	5	6	7	8
g	1000							

b) To convert a measurement in kilograms to grams, I multiply by _____.

c) Change the measurement to grams.

   i) 3 kg = _____   ii) 9 kg = _____   iii) 17 kg = _____   iv) 25 kg = _____

7. Convert the measurement in kilograms to grams. Then circle the greater measurement.

   a) 500 g   ⬭7 kg⬮   b) 8300 g   95 kg   c) 24 567 g   15 kg

   　　　　　7000 g

   d) 2222 g   2 kg   e) 60 kg   6200 g   f) 72 kg   45 203 g

8. Use the table in Question 6.

   a) Write a measurement in grams that is between 5 kg and 6 kg. _____

   b) Write a measurement in kilograms that is between 3790 g and 4258 g. _____

9. Convert the measurement in grams to a mixed measurement.

   a) 5130 g = ___5___ kg ___130___ g   b) 5217 g = _____ kg _____ g

   c) 4367 g = _____ kg _____ g   d) 4081 g = _____ kg _____ g

   e) 7006 g = _____ kg _____ g   f) 44 300 g = _____ kg _____ g

   g) 10 201 g = _____ kg _____ g   h) 100 001 g = _____ kg _____ g

10. Convert the mixed measurement to a measurement in grams.

   a) 3 kg = ___3000___ g   b) 4 kg = _____ g   c) 5 kg = _____ g

   so 3 kg 71 g   so 4 kg 510 g   so 5 kg 45 g

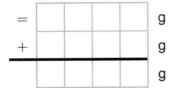

	3	0	0	0	g
+			7	1	g
	3	0	7	1	g

   d) 8 kg 128 g = _____ g e) 9 kg 237 g = _____ g f) 7 kg 3 g = _____ g

ME6-7 Mass Word Problems

> We measure mass of very small objects in **milligrams**. Write 1 **mg** for 1 milligram. 1 g = 1000 mg
>
> Here are some masses in milligrams:
>
> small ant: about 1 mg   grain of sand: about 10 mg $5 bill: 930 mg

1. Should you use milligrams or grams to measure the mass?

   a) grain of rice

   mg   g

   b) pebble

   mg   g

   c) small feather

   mg   g

> We use milligrams when we need to be precise. Doctors use milligrams for medications.

2. Circle the measurement that best fills the blank.

   a) Each pill contains _____ of vitamin C.   500 mg   500 g   500 kg

   b) A $1 coin weighs a little less than _____.   7 mg   7 g   7 kg

   c) A cup can hold _____ of flour.   125 mg   125 g

   d) An adult moose weighs about _____.   450 mg   450 g   450 kg

   e) A grain of salt weighs about _____.   5 mg   5 g   5 kg

> We measure mass of very large objects in **tonnes**. Write 1 **t** for 1 tonne. 1 tonne = 1000 kg
>
> Here are some masses in tonnes:
>
> small car: about 1 t   adult male orca: about 4 t   loaded train car: about 135 t

3. What number do you multiply by to change the measurement?

   a) from tonnes to kilograms: _____

   b) from kilograms to grams: _____

   c) from grams to milligrams: _____

   BONUS ▶ from tonnes to grams: _____

4. Convert the measurements and fill in the table.

a)

kg	g
3	
14	
147	
	5000

b)

g	mg
6	
20	
582	
	70 000

c)

t	kg
7	
83	
705	
	400 000

5. Two newborn polar bear cubs weigh 450 g each. Their mother is 300 times as heavy as both cubs together. How much does the mother bear weigh? Use the best unit to represent her mass.

6. a) Eight squash seeds weigh about 1 g. How many milligrams does one squash seed weigh?

b) A pack of squash seeds weighs 5 g. About how many seeds are in the pack?

c) Cucumber seeds weigh about 30 mg each. Tomato seeds weigh about 3 mg each.

David buys 100 tomato seeds, 50 cucumber seeds, and 20 squash seeds. How much do his seeds weigh altogether?

7. A mail carrier has 6 kg of letters in her bag. Each letter has a mass of about 20 g. About how many letters does she have in the bag?

8. An average honey bee weighs about 90 mg. There are about 50 000 bees in a beehive.

a) What is the total mass of bees in a beehive?

b) There are 12 beehives on a honey farm. What is the total mass in kilograms of bees on the farm?

c) Each bee produces about 450 mg of honey in a year. About how much honey in kilograms do the bees on the farm produce in a year?

9. An empty moving truck weighs 3980 kg. The driver weighs 93 kg, and his partner weighs 87 kg. They load the truck with 2650 kg of furniture and boxes.

a) Can they drive the truck over a bridge that allows only vehicles that weigh 7 tonnes or less? Explain.

b) They pick up three more passengers that weigh about 80 kg each. Can they drive the truck over the bridge? Explain.

10. The table shows the masses of several of the heaviest and lightest animals on Earth.

Animal	Mass
African bush elephant	6350 kg
Bee hummingbird	1 g 600 mg
Blue whale	140 tonnes
Common ostrich	120 kg
Elephant beetle	50 g
Pygmy shrew	1800 mg

a) Order the animals from heaviest to lightest.

b) How much heavier is the heaviest animal than the lightest animal?

c) Create your own problem using the information in the table.

G6-1 Angles

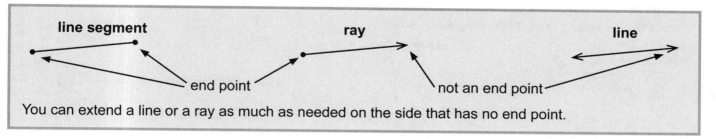

You can extend a line or a ray as much as needed on the side that has no end point.

1. Identify the picture as a line, line segment, or ray. Then write the number of end points.

a)

_____

_____ end points

b)

_____

_____ end points

c)

_____

_____ end point

2. Extend the ray at one end.

a)

b)

c)

When two rays have the same end point, they form an **angle**.
You do not have to draw a dot to show the common end point.

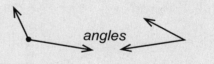

3. Circle the pictures that show angles.

An angle has a **vertex** and **arms**. You can extend the arms as much as needed without changing the angle.

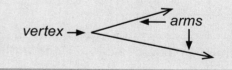

4. Circle the vertex and extend the arms of each angle.

The **size** of an angle is how much you need to turn one arm to get to the other arm.
The **arc** (⌒) shows how much you need to turn.

smaller 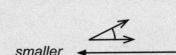   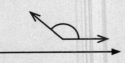 *larger*

5. Circle the larger angle in the pair.

a)

b)

c)

d)

These angles are the same size—you need to turn the *same* amount to get from one arm to the other arm of both angles. One angle looks larger because the rays extend farther.

6. Are the angles the same? Extend the arms that look shorter to help you decide.

a)

b)

7. Circle the larger angle. Then extend the arms that are shorter to check your answer.

a)

b)

Square corners are called **right angles**.

Straight angles are made by two opposite rays that are part of the same line.

straight angle

8. Circle the angles that are smaller than a right angle. Cross out the angles that are larger than a straight angle.

G6-2 Measuring Angles

We measure angles in **degrees**.
Example: This angle measures 1 degree.

1. What is the size of the angle?

a)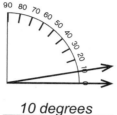

__10 degrees__

b)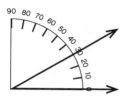

_____

c)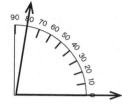

_____

We use a small raised circle after the number instead of the word "degree": 1 degree = 1°.
A right angle measures 90°. A straight angle measures 180°.

2. Identify the angle as "less than 90°" or "more than 90°."

a)

__less than 90°__

b)

_____

c)

_____

d)

_____

e)

_____

f)

_____

Acute angles are less than a right angle. They measure between 0° and 90°. **Obtuse angles** are greater than a right angle and smaller than a straight angle. They measure between 90° and 180°.

3. Identify the angle as "acute" or "obtuse."

a)

_____

b)

_____

c)

_____

d)

_____

e)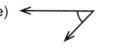

_____

f)

_____

4. Identify the angle measure as that of an "acute" or "obtuse" angle.

a) 55° _____

b) 130° _____

c) 66° _____

d) 93° _____

e) 178° _____

f) 19° _____

To measure an angle, we use a **protractor**.

A protractor has 180 subdivisions of 1° around its curved side.
It has two scales, to measure angles starting from either side.

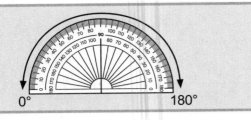

0°   180°

5. Identify the angle as "acute" or "obtuse."
   Circle the two numbers that the arm of the angle passes through.
   Choose the correct angle measure. (Example: If you said the angle is acute,
   choose the number that is less than 90.)

a)

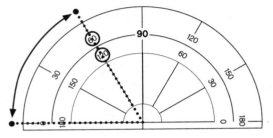

The angle is _____*acute*_____.

The angle measures ___*60°*___.

b)

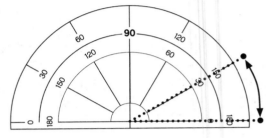

The angle is _____.

The angle measures _____.

c)

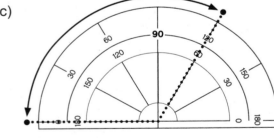

The angle is _____.

The angle measures _____.

d)

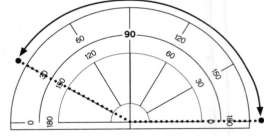

The angle is _____.

The angle measures _____.

6. Identify the angle as "acute" or "obtuse." Then write the measure of the angle.

a)

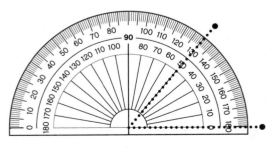

_____ , _____

b)

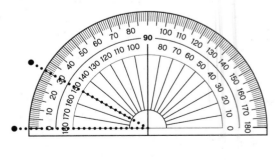

_____ , _____

7. Identify the angle as "acute" or "obtuse." Then write the measure of the angle.

a)

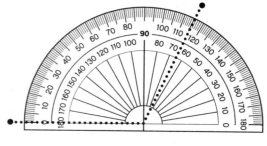

_____ , _____

b)

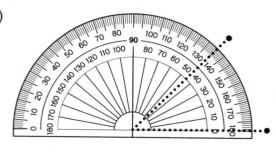

_____ , _____

c)

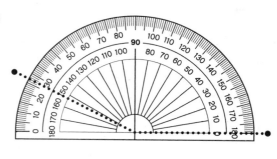

_____ , _____

d)

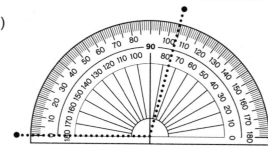

_____ , _____

Each protractor has a **base line** and an **origin**.

To measure an angle, line up the base line of the protractor with one arm of the angle.
Place the origin of the protractor on the vertex of the angle.

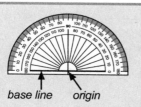

base line   origin

---

8. a) In which picture is the protractor placed correctly? _____

A.

B.

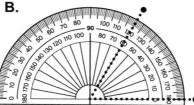

C.

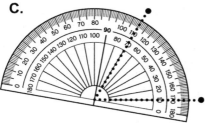

b) What is wrong with the other pictures?

9. Measure the angle using a protractor. Extend the arms if needed.

a)

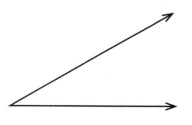

_____

b)

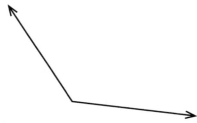

_____

c)

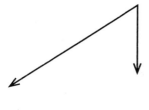

_____

G6-3 Estimating Angles

1. Measure the angle using a protractor. Write the measure beside the angle.
Extend the arms if needed.

a)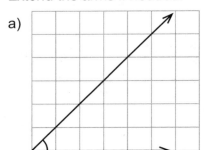

b)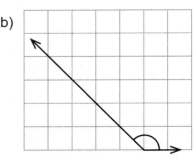

c)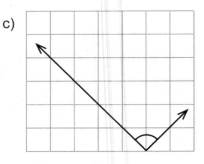

2. Use the grid to estimate the angle. Then measure the angle to check your estimate.

a)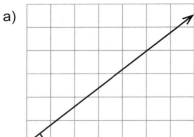

Estimate: _____

Actual: _____

b)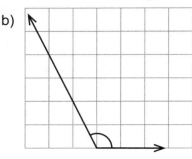

Estimate: _____

Actual: _____

c)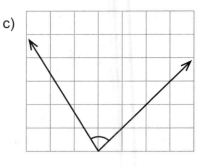

Estimate: _____

Actual: _____

d)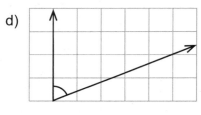

Estimate: _____

Actual: _____

e)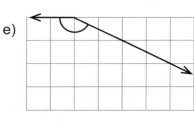

Estimate: _____

Actual: _____

BONUS ▶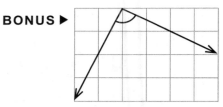

Estimate: _____

Actual: _____

Reflex angles are larger than straight angles. Reflex angles measure between 180° and 360°.

3. Circle the reflex angles.

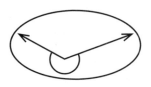

4. A full turn is 360°. Estimate the measure of the acute or obtuse angle. Then subtract to estimate the measure of the reflex angle.

a)

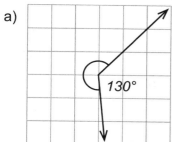

Estimate: _360° − 130°_

= _230°_

b)

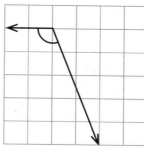

Estimate: _____

= _____

c)

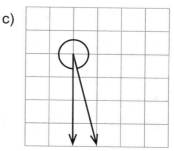

Estimate: _____

= _____

5. Estimate the measure of the angle. Then use a protractor to check.

a)

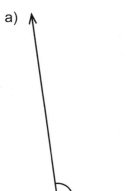

Estimate: _____

Actual: _____

b)

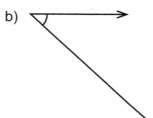

Estimate: _____

Actual: _____

c)

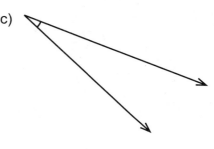

Estimate: _____

Actual: _____

6. The shaded angle measures 10°.

a) Use estimation to draw a ray that makes an angle of 20° with the top arm of the angle. Do not use a protractor.

b) Measure the angle you created. Was your estimate close?

_____

7. Alex divides the large angle into equal smaller angles. The first smaller angle is shaded.

a) Estimate the size of the remaining angle. _____

b) Estimate the size of the shaded angle. _____

c) How many smaller angles will fit into the larger angle? _____

d) Measure the angles to check your estimates.

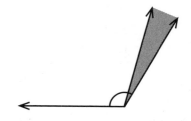

G6-4 Constructing Angles

We use capital letters to name points.
We use end points to name line segments.

line segment *AB*
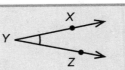

1. a) Measure the line segment *CD* to the nearest millimetre.

   CD = _____

   b) Draw a line segment *EF* that is 4 cm long.

When naming an angle, write the vertex in the middle.

Example: This angle is named ∠XYZ or ∠ZYX.

2. Circle the vertex. Then name the angle.

   a)
   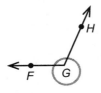
   ∠ _FGH_

   b)

   ∠ _____

   c)
   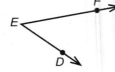
   ∠ _____

3. a) What is half of 90? _____

   b) One arm of the angle is drawn. Use a ruler and the grid to draw the angle of the given measure. Label the angle.

   i) ∠ABC = 90°
   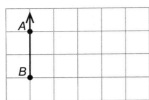

   ii) ∠BCD = 45°
   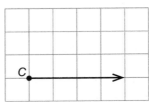

   iii) ∠EFG = 90°
   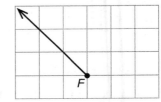

   c) Use a protractor to check your work in part b).

When there is no chance of confusion, you can name an angle with the vertex letter.

4. Circle the vertices of the angles you can name using only the vertex letter. Name the angles.

   a)
   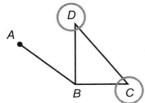
   _∠D, ∠C_

   b)
   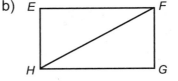
   _____

   c)
   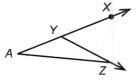
   _____

To draw a 60° angle:

Step 1: Draw a ray. Place the protractor as shown.

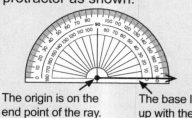

The origin is on the end point of the ray.

The base line lines up with the ray.

Step 2: Make a mark at 60°.

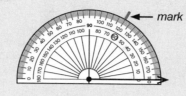

← mark

Step 3: Use a ruler to draw a ray from the end point to the mark.

← mark

5. Place the protractor as shown in Step 1. Which mark lines up with the given angle?

a) 60°

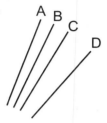

b) 140°

6. Finish drawing the angle.

a) 130°

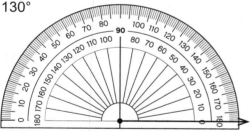

b) 75°

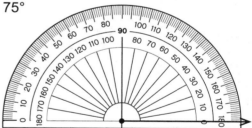

7. Use a protractor to finish drawing the angle.

a) 40°

b) 160°

8. Use a protractor to draw the angle. Label the angle.

a) ∠$ABC = 35°$ b) ∠$DEF = 135°$ c) ∠$LOM = 72°$ d) ∠$UVW = 116°$

G6-5 Angles in Polygons

1. Extend the arms of the angle marked with an arc. Then measure the angle.

   a)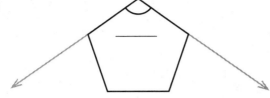

   b)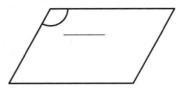

   c)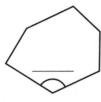

   d)

> In Question 1 you measured one **interior angle** in each polygon.
> The interior angles in a polygon are shaded in this picture.

2. Label the interior angles in the polygon. Mark each right angle with a small square, each acute angle with an *A*, each obtuse angle with an *O*, and each reflex angle with an *R*.

   a)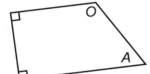

   b)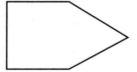

   c)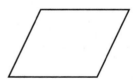

   d)

   e)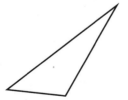

   f)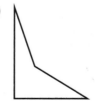

   g)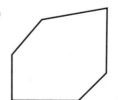

   h)

3. Measure the angles in the triangle.

   a)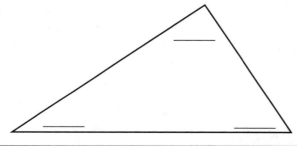

   b)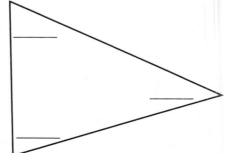

4. a) Draw a triangle with two 45° angles and the side between them as shown.

i)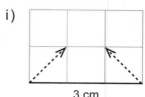

3 cm

ii)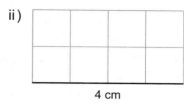

4 cm

b) Measure the third angle in the triangles you drew.

i) _____

ii) _____

5. Construct a triangle with sides of 5 cm and 4 cm and an angle of 50° between them by following the steps below.

a) Use a ruler to mark a line segment 5 cm long on the line at right. Label the end points A and B.

b) Use the line segment from part a) and a protractor to construct $\angle A = 50°$.

c) Mark point C on the ray so that $AC = 4$ cm.

d) Draw line segment BC.

⟵⟶

6. Construct a quadrilateral with 3 sides of 55 mm and angles of 60° and 120° by following the steps below.

a) Draw $\angle D = 60°$.

b) Mark points E and G on the sides of the angle so that $DE = 55$ mm and $DG = 55$ mm.

c) Draw $\angle DEF = 120°$. Mark point F so that $EF = 55$ mm.

d) Draw line segment FG.

e) Measure line segment FG, $\angle F$, and $\angle G$. What do you notice?

_____

_____

7. Use the methods from Questions 5 and 6 to draw the polygon.

a) triangle HIJ so that $HI = IJ = 43$ mm, $\angle HIJ = 25°$

b) quadrilateral $KLMN$ so that $KL = MN = 5$ cm, $LM = 6$ cm, and $\angle L = \angle M = 100°$

BONUS ▶ pentagon $PQRST$ so that all sides are 4 cm long and all angles are 108°

G6-6 Classifying Polygons

We use **hash marks** to show equal sides in polygons.
This triangle has 2 equal sides.

Opposite sides in a rectangle are equal.

 hash marks

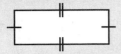

1. Measure the sides of the polygon to the closest millimetre. Mark equal sides with hash marks.

a)

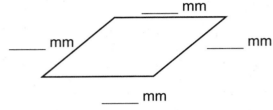

_____ mm

_____ mm

_____ mm

_____ mm

b)

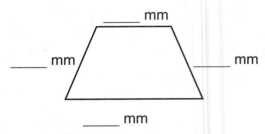

_____ mm

_____ mm

_____ mm

_____ mm

A polygon that has *all sides* the same length is called an **equilateral polygon**.

2. Measure the sides of the polygon to the closest millimetre. Measure the angles of the polygon. Colour the equilateral polygons.

a)

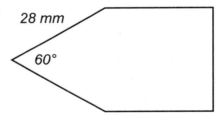

28 mm

60°

b)

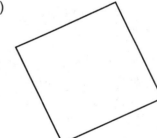

c)

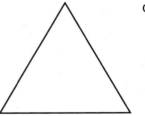

d)

e)

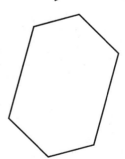

f)

Regular polygons have all sides the same length and all angles of the same measure.

3. a) Circle the regular polygons in Question 2.

b) Which polygons in Question 2 are equilateral but not regular? _____

c) Which polygons in Question 2 have all angles equal but are not regular? _____

To show angles are equal, you can mark them with arcs, double arcs, or (for right angles) small squares. This polygon has two different pairs of equal angles.

4. a) Circle the regular polygons.

   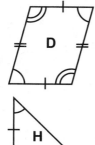

 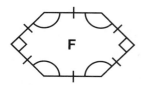

b) Sort the polygons. Some polygons will be in both rows.

Polygons with all angles equal	A,
Equilateral polygons	A,

c) Use the table above to sort the polygons into the Venn diagram.

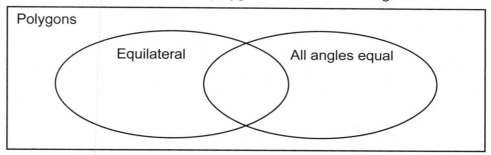

d) Which region of the Venn diagram contains all regular polygons? _____

e) Which Venn diagram will always have an empty region? Shade the region that will always be empty.

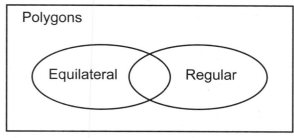 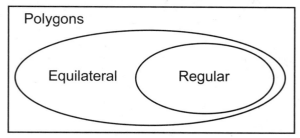

5. Use a protractor and ruler to draw the polygons.

a) Draw a triangle *ABC* with *AB* = 5 cm and ∠*A* = ∠*B* = 60°. Is *ABC* a regular triangle?

b) Draw a quadrilateral *DEFG* with *DE* = *EF* = 5 cm and ∠*D* = ∠*E* = ∠*F* = 90°. Is *DEFG* a regular quadrilateral?

c) Draw a quadrilateral *HIJK* with ∠*H* = ∠*I* = ∠*J* = 90°, so that it is not a regular quadrilateral.

G6-7 Congruence

Two shapes are **congruent** if they have the same size and shape. If you place one shape on top of the other and line them up, they will match exactly.

Congruent shapes:

Non-congruent shapes: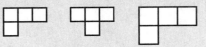

1. Circle the two congruent shapes.

a)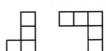

b)

c)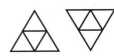

d)

Congruent polygons have sides of the same length.

Example: Triangles A and B are congruent. Triangles B and C are not congruent.

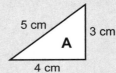 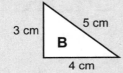 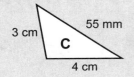

2. The two triangles shown are congruent. Mark the equal sides with hash marks. One pair of sides in part a) is marked for you.

a)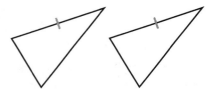

b)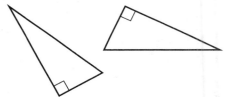

3. Triangles *ABC* and *DEF* are congruent. Which side in triangle *ABC* is equal to the given side of triangle *DEF*?

a)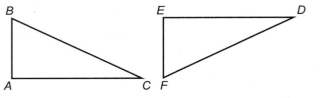

b)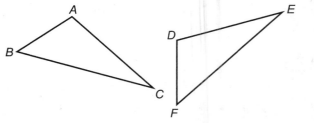

$DE = \underline{\ AC\ }$, $EF = \underline{\ \ \ \ \ \ }$, $DF = \underline{\ \ \ \ \ \ }$

$DE = \underline{\ \ \ \ \ \ }$, $EF = \underline{\ \ \ \ \ \ }$, $DF = \underline{\ \ \ \ \ \ }$

If two polygons are congruent, they have angles of the same size.

Example: Triangles A and B are congruent, so they have angles of the same size. Triangles B and C have angles of different sizes. They are not congruent.

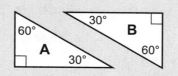 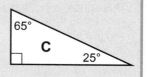

4. The triangles shown are congruent. Mark the equal angles with the same number of arcs. One pair of angles is marked for you.

a)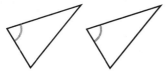

b)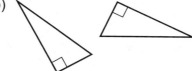

5. Triangles *ABC* and *DEF* are congruent. Which angle in triangle *ABC* is equal to the given angle of triangle *DEF*?

a)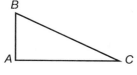

∠*D* = __∠*C*__ , ∠*E* = _____ , ∠*F* = _____

b)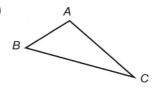

∠*D* = _____ , ∠*E* = _____ , ∠*F* = _____

To check if two polygons are congruent, imagine placing them one on top of the other, trying to make them match exactly.

Compare the angles placed one on top of the other: ∠*A* = ∠*G*, ∠*B* = ∠*F*, ∠*C* = ∠*E*.

Compare the lengths of the sides placed one on top of the other: *AB* = *GF*, *BC* = *FE*, *CA* = *EG*.

If all pairs of angles and all pairs of sides are equal, the polygons are congruent.

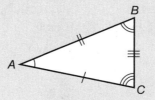 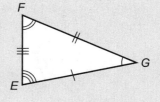

6. Are the triangles congruent? Use a ruler and a protractor to check. If yes, write the pairs of matching equal sides and matching equal angles.

a)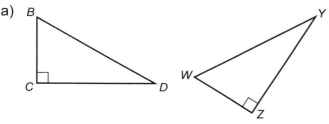

b)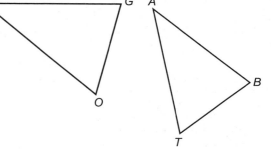

G6-8 Classifying Triangles

1. Measure and label the angles in the triangle. Extend the arms of the angles if needed.

   a)

   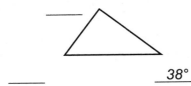

   _____ _38°_

   b)

   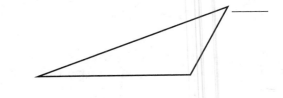

2. Mark the largest angle in the triangle with an arc.

   a) 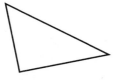   b) 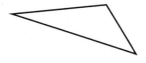   c)   d)

You can classify triangles by the size of the largest angle.

acute-angled or **acute** triangle

The largest angle is acute.

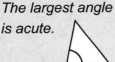

right-angled or **right** triangle

The largest angle is right.

obtuse-angled or **obtuse** triangle

The largest angle is obtuse.

---

3. Mark the largest angle in the triangle with an arc. Use a square corner to check if the angle is acute, right, or obtuse. Then classify the triangle.

   a)    b)   c)   d)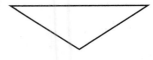

   obtuse triangle   _____   _____   _____

4. Classify the triangle.

   a) 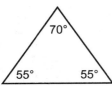   b) 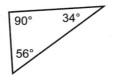   c)   d)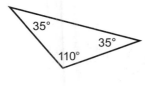

   _____   _____   _____   _____

5. Use a ruler to draw the triangle.

a) acute triangle

b) right triangle

c) obtuse triangle

d) triangle without a right angle

 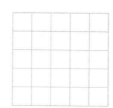  

6. How many acute angles does an acute triangle have? Explain. _____

_____

You can classify triangles by the number of *equal* sides.

isosceles triangle

At least 2 equal sides.

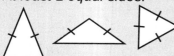

scalene triangle

No equal sides.

Isosceles triangles with 3 equal sides are called **equilateral** triangles.

---

7. Measure the sides of the triangle that seem to be equal to the nearest millimetre. Mark the equal sides. Then classify the triangle as equilateral, isosceles, or scalene.

a)

b)

c)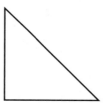

d)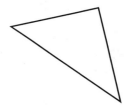

_____ _____ _____ _____

8. a) Classify the triangle as equilateral, isosceles, or scalene.

i)

ii)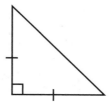

iii)

iv)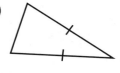

_____ _____ _____ _____

b) Classify the triangles above as acute, right, or obtuse.

i) _____ ii) _____ iii) _____ iv) _____

9. a) Mark the triangle for any equal sides, equal angles, and right angles. Use a ruler to check for equal sides. Use a protractor to check angles.

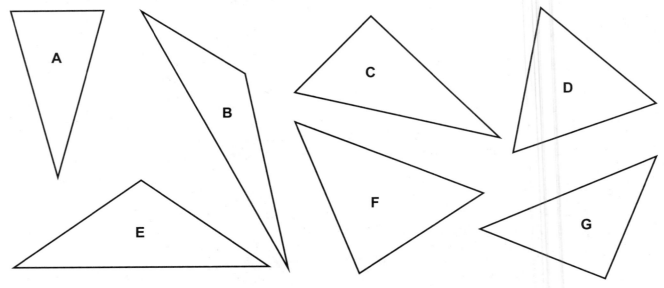

b) Classify the triangles in the tables below.

Acute-angled	
Right-angled	
Obtuse-angled	

Equilateral	
Isosceles	
Scalene	

c) Sort the triangles into 2 groups in a Venn diagram.

i)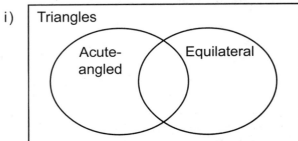

ii)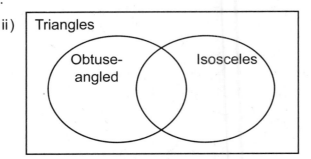

iii) Group 1: right-angled

Group 2: scalene

iv) Group 1: acute-angled

Group 2: scalene

10. In each triangle in Question 9, look at the two angles that are *not the largest*. Are they acute, right, or obtuse angles?

11. Use a ruler and protractor to construct the triangles. Use angle and side measurements to explain how the triangles you constructed are the same or different.

a) two congruent right scalene triangles that point in different directions

b) two obtuse isosceles triangles that are not congruent

1. Add the measures of the angles in the triangle.

a)

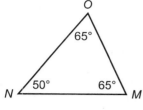

∠M + ∠N + ∠O

= _____

= _____

b)

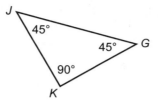

∠G + ∠J + ∠K

= _____

= _____

c)

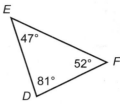

∠D + ∠E + ∠F

= _____

= _____

d)

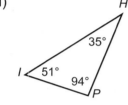

∠I + ∠P + ∠H

= _____

= _____

e)

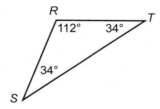

∠S + ∠R + ∠T

= _____

= _____

BONUS ▶

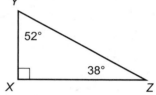

∠Z + ∠Y + ∠X

= _____

= _____

2. Measure the angles in the triangle. Then add the angles.

a)

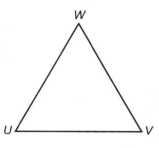

∠U = _____

∠V = _____

∠W = _____

∠U + ∠V + ∠W = _____

b)

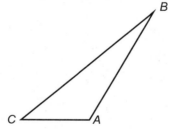

∠A = _____

∠B = _____

∠C = _____

∠A + ∠B + ∠C = _____

c)

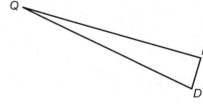

∠D = _____

∠L = _____

∠Q = _____

∠D + ∠L + ∠Q = _____

3. Look at the sum of the angles in each triangle in Questions 1 and 2. What do you notice?

_____

_____

4. Add the measures of the angles in the quadrilateral.

a)

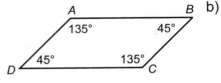

$\angle A + \angle B + \angle C + \angle D$

= _____

= _____

b)

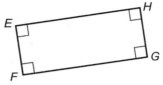

$\angle E + \angle F + \angle G + \angle H$

= _____

= _____

c)

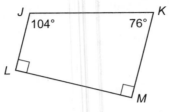

$\angle J + \angle K + \angle M + \angle L$

= _____

= _____

5. Measure the angles in the quadrilateral. Then add the angles.

a)

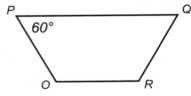

= _____

= _____

b)

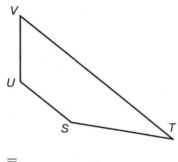

= _____

= _____

c)

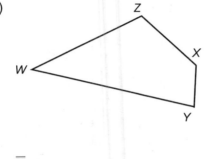

= _____

= _____

6. Look at the sum of the angles in each quadrilateral in Questions 4 and 5.

What do you notice? _____

The sum of the angles in a triangle is 180°.

The sum of the angles in a quadrilateral is 360°.

$\angle A + \angle B + \angle C = 180°$ 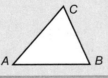 $\angle E + \angle F + \angle G + \angle H = 360°$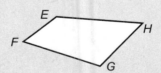

---

7. a) A triangle has an angle that measures 30° and an angle that measures 60°.
What is the measure of the third angle in the triangle?

b) A triangle has two angles of 45°. What is the measure of the third angle in the triangle?

c) A triangle has all angles equal. What is the measure of each angle?

8. a) Could a triangle ever have more than one obtuse angle? Use a sketch to explain.

b) Could a triangle ever have more than one right angle? Use a sketch to explain.

9. Use the picture to explain why the angles in a quadrilateral always add to 360°.

G6-10 Trapezoids and Parallelograms

Parallel lines are like the long, straight rails on a railroad track.
Parallel lines:

• are straight
• go in the same direction

You can extend lines in both directions as much as you want.
No matter how long they are, parallel lines will **never** meet.

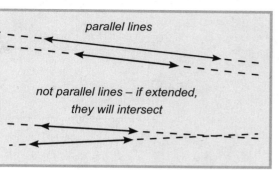

parallel lines

*not parallel lines – if extended,
they will intersect*

1. Extend the lines to check if they intersect. Then circle parallel lines.

a)   b)   c)   d)

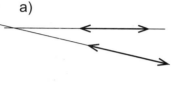   

We use arrows to mark parallel sides. If there is more than
one pair of parallel sides in a shape, use a different number
of arrows for each pair.

Example:

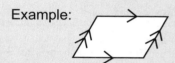

2. Mark all pairs of parallel sides in the polygon.

a)   b)   c)   d)

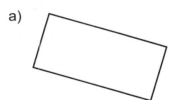   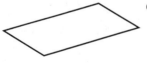      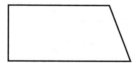

Quadrilaterals with exactly 1 pair of parallel sides are called **trapezoids**.
Quadrilaterals with 2 pairs of parallel sides are called **parallelograms**.

Trapezoids   Parallelograms

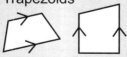

3. Mark parallel sides with arrows. Then identify the type of quadrilateral.

a)   b)   c)   d)

      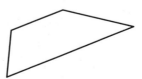   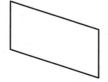

_____   _____   _____   _____

4. a) Measure the parallel sides of the quadrilaterals to the closest millimetre.

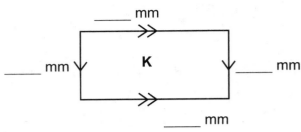

_____ mm

_____ mm **K** _____ mm

_____ mm

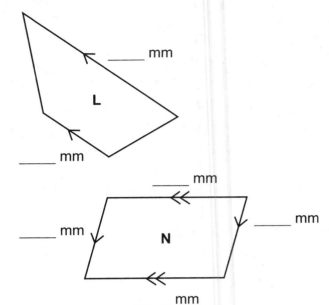

_____ mm

L

_____ mm

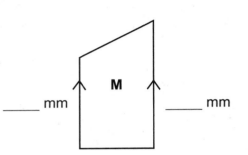

M

_____ mm _____ mm

_____ mm

_____ mm **N** _____ mm

_____ mm

b) Sort the shapes into the tables.

Parallelograms	
Trapezoids	

Parallel sides are equal	
Parallel sides are not equal	

c) What do you notice about the tables? _____
_____

d) One pair of parallel sides is marked. Use your answer in part c) to check if the other pair of sides is parallel. Then identify the type of quadrilateral.

i)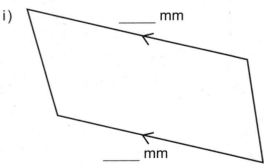

_____ mm

_____ mm

_____

ii)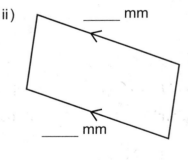

_____ mm

_____ mm

_____

5. Rob thinks that the quadrilateral shown is a parallelogram because the opposite sides are equal. Is he correct? Explain.

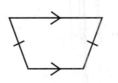

_____

_____

_____

> *Parallel* sides of a parallelogram are always equal. *Parallel* sides of a trapezoid always have different lengths.

6. a) The equal sides are not marked on two of the quadrilaterals. Mark them.

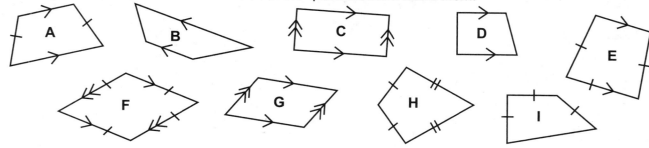

b) Colour the parallelograms red and colour the trapezoids blue.

c) Sort the quadrilaterals.

d) What is the largest number of equal sides a parallelogram can have? _____

e) What is the largest number of equal sides a trapezoid can have? _____

No equal sides	
Exactly 2 equal sides	
Exactly 3 equal sides	
4 equal sides (equilateral)	
2 different pairs of equal sides	

7. A quadrilateral has four equal sides.

a) Can it be a parallelogram? _____   b) Can it be a trapezoid? _____

> An **isosceles trapezoid** has equal opposite non-parallel sides.
>
> A **right trapezoid** has two right angles.

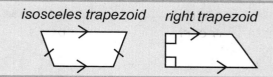

isosceles trapezoid   right trapezoid

8. a) Mark the right angles in the quadrilaterals in Question 6. Use a square corner to check.

b) Which quadrilaterals in Question 6 are right trapezoids? _____

c) Which quadrilaterals in Question 6 are isosceles trapezoids? _____

9. a) Measure the angles of the parallelogram.

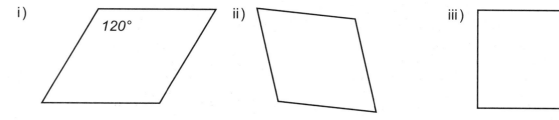

i) 120°   ii)   iii)

b) What do you notice about the opposite angles in a parallelogram? _____

c) Look at the trapezoids in Question 6. Do they have equal opposite angles? _____

G6-11 Symmetry

A **line of symmetry** divides a figure into two parts that are the same size and shape. The two parts match exactly if you fold the figure along the line of symmetry.

The dotted line is a line of symmetry

The dotted line is *not* a line of symmetry.

1. Is the dashed line a line of symmetry? Write "yes" or "no."

a)

yes

b)

no

c)

yes

d)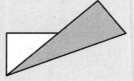

no

2. a) Does the shape have a line of symmetry? If yes, draw it. Use a ruler.

A.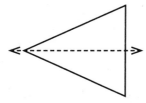

yes

B.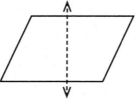

no

C.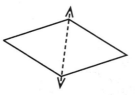

yes

D.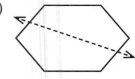

no

b) Draw all the lines of symmetry in the shape. Use a ruler.

E.

F.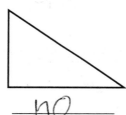

G.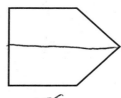

H.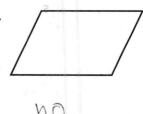

c) Sort the shapes by the number of lines of symmetry.

Number of lines of symmetry	0	1	2	More than 2
Shapes				

3. a) Use a ruler to draw the line of symmetry in the pentagon.

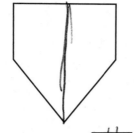

b) Measure the sides and the angles of the pentagon. What do you notice?

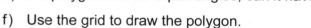

c) The dashed line is a line of symmetry. Without measuring, mark the equal sides and the equal angles in the hexagon.

d) If a polygon has no equal sides, can it have a line of symmetry? __?__

e) If a polygon has no equal angles, can it have a line of symmetry? __?__

f) Use the grid to draw the polygon.

   i) a quadrilateral without lines of symmetry   ii) a triangle with exactly 1 line of symmetry

If you can turn a shape less than a full turn (360°) around its centre and it looks the same, the shape has **rotational symmetry**. Some shapes can have both rotational and line symmetry.

Rotational symmetry:
If you turn the shape a quarter turn, it looks the same.

Rotational and line symmetry:
If you turn the shape half a turn (180°), it looks the same.

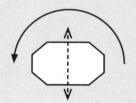

No rotational symmetry:
Only a full turn (360°) brings the shape back.

---

4. Circle the shapes that have rotational symmetry. Shade the shapes that have line symmetry.

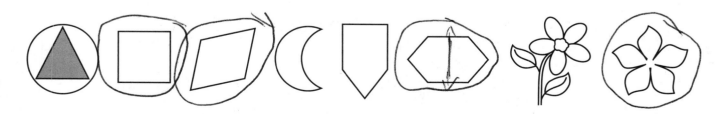

The **order of rotational symmetry** is the number of times a shape fits onto itself during one full (360°) rotation. To find the order of rotational symmetry:

Step 1: Mark a corner of the shape.

Step 2: Turn the shape and count how many times the shape fits onto itself during a full turn (360°).

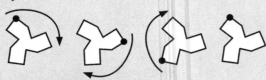

The shape in the picture fits onto itself 3 times. It has **rotational symmetry of order 3**.

5. a) Find the order of rotational symmetry of the polygon.

A.   B.    C.    D.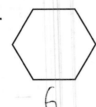

___3___   ___5___   ___2___   ___6___

E.   F. 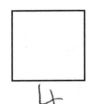   G. 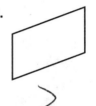   H.

___5___   ___4___   ___2___   ___0___

I. 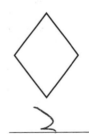   J. 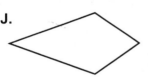   K.   L.

___2___   ___0___   ___4___   ___0___

b) Sort the shapes by the order of rotational symmetry.

Order of rotational symmetry	1	2	3	4	More than 4
Shapes	H, L, J	C, G, I	A	F, K	B, D, E

c) Polygons with rotational symmetry of order 1 have **no rotational symmetry**.

Which polygons have no rotational symmetry but have a line of symmetry? H, J

d) Which polygons have rotational symmetry but have no line of symmetry? G, K

e) Which polygons have no rotational symmetry and no line of symmetry? L

> **BONUS ▶** Amy thinks the order of rotational symmetry is always less than or equal to the number of lines of symmetry. Is she correct? Explain. ✗

G. ▱ 2 rota.   0 lines 0
sem g.

Geometry 6-11

6. a) Draw all the lines of symmetry in the regular polygon.

M.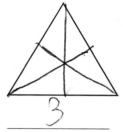

_____ 3 _____

N.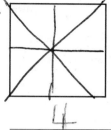

_____ 4 _____

O.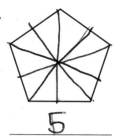

_____ 5 _____

P.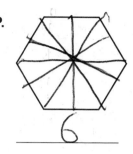

_____ 6 _____

b) Write the order of symmetry below the shape.

c) Fill in the table.

Shape	M	N	O	P
Number of sides	3	4	5	6
Number of lines of symmetry	3	4	5	6
Order of rotational symmetry	3	4	5	6

d) Predict the number of lines of symmetry and order of rotational symmetry in a regular octagon. Check your prediction.

Number of lines of symmetry = ___8___

Order of rotational symmetry = ___8___

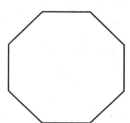

e) Predict the number of lines of symmetry and the order of rotational symmetry for a regular polygon with 20 sides.

Number of lines of symmetry = ___20___

Order of rotational symmetry = ___20___

7. Use grid paper and a ruler.

a) i) Draw a quadrilateral that has 1 line of symmetry and no rotational symmetry.

ii) Draw a quadrilateral that has 2 lines of symmetry.

iii) Draw a quadrilateral that has 4 lines of symmetry.

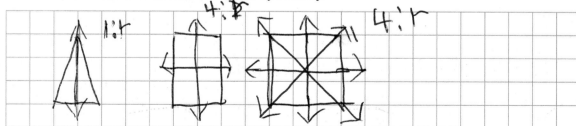

b) What is the order of rotational symmetry of the polygons you drew in part a)?

c) Draw a polygon that has 4 lines of symmetry and rotational symmetry of order 4, but is not a regular polygon. Hint: You cannot make it a quadrilateral.

G6-12 Classifying Quadrilaterals

1. a) Trapezoids have _____ of parallel sides.

    b) Circle two angles that you would use to explain why *ABCD* is a trapezoid.

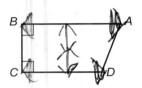

2. a) A rectangle is a quadrilateral with _____ right angles. Mark the right angles in rectangle *EFGH*.

    b) Are all rectangles also parallelograms? _____

    c) Circle two angles that you would use to explain why *EFGH* has parallel sides *EF* and *GH*.

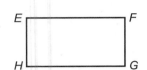

3. a) Which Venn diagram will always have an empty region? Cross out that diagram.

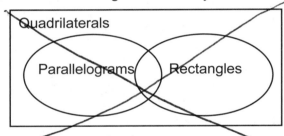
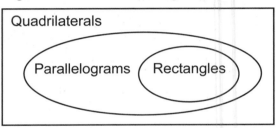

    b) Sketch a quadrilateral in every region of the diagram that is not crossed out.

Equilateral polygons have all sides equal. A **rhombus** is an equilateral parallelogram.

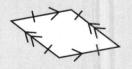

4. a) Measure the sides of the parallelogram to the closest millimetre. Then decide if it is a rhombus.

    i) 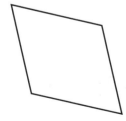   ii) 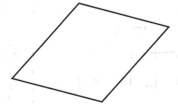   iii)

    _____   _____   _____

    b) Opposite angles in a parallelogram are equal.
        Should opposite angles in a rhombus be equal? _____

    c) To check your prediction from part b), measure the angles in any rhombus above.

5. a) Sketch a quadrilateral in each region of the Venn diagram below.

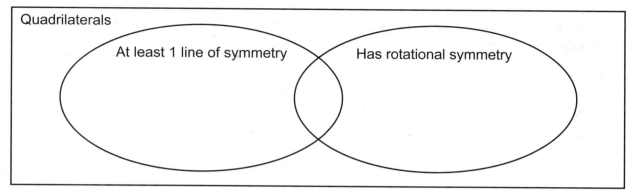

Quadrilaterals

At least 1 line of symmetry

Has rotational symmetry

b) Which region of the Venn diagram contains all quadrilaterals of the given type?

   i)   rectangles _____

   ii) rhombuses _____

   iii) right trapezoids _____

   iv) squares _____

6. a) Explain why all rectangles are also parallelograms.

b) A rectangle has one side 15 cm and another side 6 cm. What are the lengths of the other two sides? Explain. Use the word "parallelogram" in your explanation.

7. The sum of the angles in a quadrilateral is always 360°.

a) Yu thinks that any quadrilateral with 4 equal angles should be a rectangle. Is she correct? Explain.

b) Explain why there cannot be a quadrilateral with exactly 3 right angles.

BONUS ▶ Explain why any parallelogram that has at least 2 right angles has to be a rectangle.

8. a) Is any square also a parallelogram? Explain.

b) Is any square also a rhombus? Explain.

c) Can a square also be a trapezoid? Explain.

d) Shade the region in the Venn diagram where all squares will be.

e) Can a polygon be in the shaded region but not be a square? If yes, sketch it. If no, explain why not.

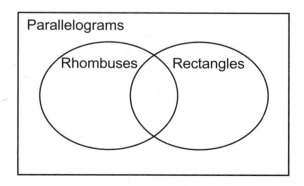

Parallelograms

Rhombuses   Rectangles

NS6-18 Lowest Common Multiples (LCMs)

The **whole numbers** are the numbers 0, 1, 2, 3, and so on. The **multiples** of a whole number are the numbers you get by multiplying the number by another whole number.

Examples:

The multiples of 2 are $2 \times 0 = \mathbf{0}$ $2 \times 1 = \mathbf{2}$ $2 \times 2 = \mathbf{4}$ $2 \times 3 = \mathbf{6}$ $2 \times 4 = \mathbf{8}$ ...

The multiples of 3 are $3 \times 0 = \mathbf{0}$ $3 \times 1 = \mathbf{3}$ $3 \times 2 = \mathbf{6}$ $3 \times 3 = \mathbf{9}$ $3 \times 4 = \mathbf{12}$ ...

1. a) Skip count to write the multiples of 3 up to 3×10.

   __0__ , __3__ , _____ , _____ , _____ , _____ , _____ , _____ , _____ , _____ , _____

   b) Use your answers in part a) to circle the multiples of 3.

   12   17   22   24   25   27

A number is a **common multiple** of two numbers if it is a multiple of both of them.

2. Mark the multiples of the numbers on the number lines. Then write their common multiples.

   a) Which numbers are common multiples of both 3 and 4?

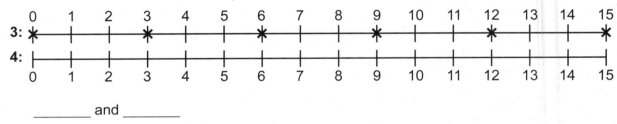

   _____ and _____

   b) Which numbers are common multiples of both 2 and 3?

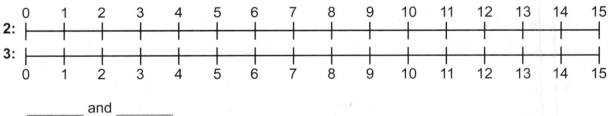

   _____ and _____

   c) Which numbers are common multiples of 3, 4, and 6?

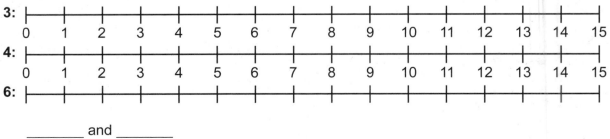

   _____ and _____

3. List the multiples of the given numbers, up to 15 times each number. Then write the first two common multiples, not including 0.

a) 3 and 4

   3: _0, 3, 6, 9, 12, 15, 18, 21, 24, 27, 30, 33, 36, 39, 42, 45_

   4: _____

   The first two common multiples are _____ and _____.

b) 2 and 3

   2: _____

   3: _____

   The first two common multiples are _____ and _____.

c) 3 and 5   d) 2 and 5   e) 2, 3, and 4   f) 2, 4, and 6

The number 0 is a multiple of every number. The **lowest common multiple (LCM)** of two numbers is the smallest whole number (not 0) that is a multiple of both numbers.

---

4. Find the lowest common multiple of the given numbers.

a) 4 and 10   b) 3 and 6   c) 4 and 6

   4: *4, 8, 12, 16, 20*   **3:**   **4:**

   10: *10, 20*   **6:**   **6:**

   LCM = _____   LCM = _____   LCM = _____

d) 5 and 10   e) 6 and 8   f) 5 and 7

   5:   **6:**   **5:**

   10:   **8:**   **7:**

   LCM = _____   LCM = _____   LCM = _____

g) 8 and 10   h) 8 and 12   i) 8 and 16

5. Find the LCM of the number and itself.

a) 3 and 3 _____   b) 4 and 4 _____   c) 5 and 5 _____

BONUS ▶ The LCM of 183 and 183 is _____.

To find the lowest common multiple of two numbers, write the first few multiples of the *larger* number until you see one that is also a multiple of the smaller number:

Example: Find the LCM of 3 and 5.

The first few multiples of 5 are 5, 10, and 15. ⟵ Stop here because 15 is a multiple of 3.

6. Find the lowest common multiple.

a) 6 and 10

10, 20, 30

LCM = ___30___

b) 9 and 12

LCM = _____

c) 7 and 10

LCM = _____

d) 6 and 9

LCM = _____

e) 6 and 15

LCM = _____

f) 8 and 9

LCM = _____

g) 5 and 8

LCM = _____

h) 3 and 6

LCM = _____

7. a) Write the LCM of the given pair of numbers.

i) 2 and 3 _____   ii) 2 and 4 _____   iii) 2 and 5 _____   iv) 2 and 6 _____

v) 2 and 7 _____   vi) 2 and 8 _____   vii) 2 and 9 _____   viii) 2 and 10 _____

b) For which numbers in part a) is the LCM of 2 and the number equal to the number itself?

_____ , _____ , _____ , and _____

c) What is the LCM of 2 and 184? How do you know? _____

_____

NS6-19 Factors

There are only three ways to write 4 as a product of two whole numbers:

$$1 \times 4 = 4 \qquad 2 \times 2 = 4 \qquad 4 \times 1 = 4$$

The numbers that appear in the products are called the **factors** of 4.

The factors of 4 are the numbers 1, 2, and 4.

1. Write the number that makes the equation true. If no number makes the equation true, write "✗" in the box.

   a) $3 \times \boxed{4} = 12$ b) $4 \times \boxed{✗} = 14$ c) $2 \times \boxed{} = 16$ d) $3 \times \boxed{} = 10$

2. Write "yes" or "no." Then use your answers to Question 1 to explain your answer.

   a) Is 3 a factor of 12? ____Yes____ because ____4 makes the equation true____.

   b) Is 4 a factor of 14? ____No____ because ____no number makes the equation true____.

   c) Is 2 a factor of 16? _____ because _____.

   d) Is 3 a factor of 10? _____ because _____.

3. Write the number that makes the equation true. If no number makes the equation true, write "✗" in the box. Then list the factors of the number.

   a) Find the factors of 6.

   $1 \times \boxed{6} = 6$

   $2 \times \boxed{3} = 6$

   $3 \times \boxed{2} = 6$

   $4 \times \boxed{✗} = 6$

   $5 \times \boxed{✗} = 6$

   $6 \times \boxed{1} = 6$

   ____1, 2, 3, 6____

   b) Find the factors of 8.

   $1 \times \boxed{} = 8$

   $2 \times \boxed{} = 8$

   $3 \times \boxed{} = 8$

   $4 \times \boxed{} = 8$

   $5 \times \boxed{} = 8$

   $6 \times \boxed{} = 8$

   $7 \times \boxed{} = 8$

   $8 \times \boxed{} = 8$

   _____

   c) Find the factors of 9.

   $1 \times \boxed{} = 9$

   $2 \times \boxed{} = 9$

   $3 \times \boxed{} = 9$

   $4 \times \boxed{} = 9$

   $5 \times \boxed{} = 9$

   $6 \times \boxed{} = 9$

   $7 \times \boxed{} = 9$

   $8 \times \boxed{} = 9$

   $9 \times \boxed{} = 9$

   _____

The numbers 2 and 3 are a **factor pair** of 6 because $2 \times 3 = 6$.

4. List the factor pairs of the number. List each pair only once.

   a) 6

   ___1___ and ___6___

   ___2___ and ___3___

   b) 8

   _____ and _____

   _____ and _____

   c) 9

   _____ and _____

   _____ and _____

5. Abella lists the factor pairs of 10 by using the chart on the right. When a number is not a factor, she writes an "✗" in the second column.

First Factor	Second Factor
1	10
2	5
3	✗
4	✗
5	2
6	✗
7	✗
8	✗
9	✗
10	1

   a) Why didn't Abella list 11 as a first factor?

   _____

   b) Use Abella's chart to write the factors of 10.

   _____ , _____ , _____ , _____

   c) Use Abella's chart to write the factor pairs of 10.

   _____ and _____   _____ and _____

6. a) Use Abella's method to find all the factor pairs of 12.

First Factor	Second Factor
1	
2	
3	
4	
5	
6	
7	
8	
9	
10	
11	
12	

   Factor pairs of 12:

   _____ and _____

   _____ and _____

   _____ and _____

   b) Write "bigger" or "smaller" in the blanks:
   As you go down the chart, the first factor gets

   _____ and the second

   factor gets _____.

7. Use Abella's method to find all the factor pairs of the number.

   a) 14   b) 15   c) 16   d) 18   e) 20   f) 24   g) 25

NS6-20 A Shorter Way to Find Factors

> **REMINDER ▶** You can write a division statement with remainder 0 for every multiplication.
>
> Example: $2 \times 7 = 14$, so $14 \div 2 = 7 \text{ R } 0$

1. Write a division equation with remainder 0 for the multiplication equation.

   a) $4 \times 3 = 12$, so ___$12 \div 4 = 3 \text{ R } 0$___   b) $7 \times 4 = 28$, so _____

   c) $3 \times 6 = 18$, so _____   d) $3 \times 4 = 12$, so _____

You can use division to check for factors.

Example: 3 is a factor of 6 because $6 \div 3$ has remainder 0.

---

2. Use division to answer the question.

   a) $16 \div 8 =$ _____ R _____   b) $14 \div 5 =$ _____ R _____

   Is 8 a factor of 16? _____   Is 5 a factor of 14? _____

   c) $34 \div 4 =$ _____ R _____   d) $24 \div 3 =$ _____ R _____

   Is 4 a factor of 34? _____   Is 3 a factor of 24? _____

   e) $63 \div 7 =$ _____ R _____   f) $54 \div 8 =$ _____ R _____

   Is 7 a factor of 63? _____   Is 8 a factor of 54? _____

3. Use long division to check if 6 is a factor.

   a) 96   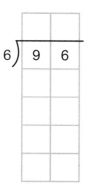   b) 84   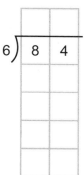   c) 72

   Is 6 a factor of 96? _____   Is 6 a factor of 84? _____   Is 6 a factor of 72? _____

   d) 80   e) 92   f) 78

4. Use long division to check if the number is a factor.

   a) Is 7 is a factor of 84?   b) Is 4 a factor of 94?   c) Is 3 a factor of 87?

5. Use the top half of the chart to finish the bottom half.

a) 18

First Factor	Second Factor
1	18
2	9
3	6
6	3
	2
	1

b) 30

First Factor	Second Factor
1	30
2	15
3	10
5	6
	5
	3
	2
	1

c) 36

First Factor	Second Factor
1	36
2	18
3	12
4	9
6	6

To list all the factors of a given number, stop when you get a number that is already part of a factor pair.

6. Make a chart to find all the factor pairs. There might be more rows than you need in the chart.

a) 20

First Factor	Second Factor
1	20
2	10
4	5
5	STOP

b) 81

First Factor	Second Factor
1	81
3	27
9	9
STOP	

c) 28

First Factor	Second Factor

d) 42

First Factor	Second Factor

e) 36

First Factor	Second Factor

f) 99

First Factor	Second Factor

NS6-21 Greatest Common Factors (GCFs)

1. Place the numbers in the Venn diagram. Cross out the numbers as you place them.

a) ~~1~~ ~~2~~ ~~3~~ ~~4~~ ~~5~~ 6 7 8 9

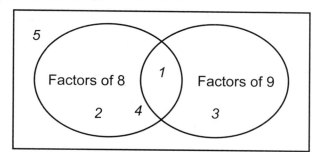

b) 1 2 3 4 5 6 7 8 9 10 11 12

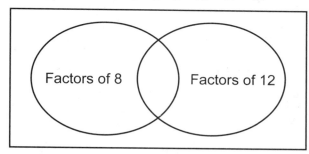

c) 1 2 3 4 5 6 7 8 9

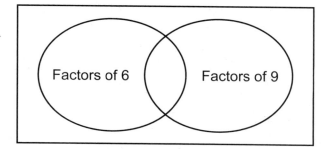

d) 1 2 3 4 5 6 7 8

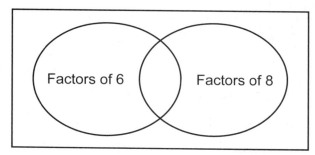

2. What number is a factor of every number? _____

> The **greatest common factor (GCF)** of two numbers is the greatest number that is a factor of both numbers.

3. a) In what region of each Venn diagram above does the greatest common factor occur?

   _____

   b) Find the greatest common factor of the two numbers.

   i) 8 and 9 ⬚   ii) 8 and 12 ⬚   iii) 6 and 9 ⬚   iv) 6 and 8 ⬚

4. a) Find and list all the factors of the number. You can make a chart in your notebook if it helps.

   i) 33   ii) 55   iii) 60

   _____1, 3, 11, 33_____   _____   _____

   _____   _____   _____

   b) Use your answers in part a) to find the greatest common factor of the two numbers.

   i) 33 and 55 _____   ii) 33 and 60 _____   iii) 55 and 60 _____

5. Find the GCF and LCM.

a) 6 and 10

GCF = ___2___

LCM = ___30___

b) 5 and 10

GCF = _____

LCM = _____

c) 6 and 15

GCF = _____

LCM = _____

d) 8 and 12

GCF = _____

LCM = _____

e) 5 and 8

f) 15 and 20

g) 12 and 14

h) 20 and 30

6. a) List the factors of 6.

_____ , _____ , _____ , and _____

b) List the first four multiples of 6, not including 0.

_____ , _____ , _____ , and _____

c) What number is both a factor and a multiple of 6? _____

7. a) List the factors of 12.

_____ , _____ , _____ , _____ , _____ , and _____

b) Write "more" or "less." All the factors of 12 except for 12 itself are _____ than 6.

c) Write "more" or "less." All the multiples of 12 except for 0 and 12 itself are _____ than 12.

d) Is any number both a factor and a multiple of 12? _____

BONUS ▶

a) What is the LCM of 10 and 10? _____

b) What is the GCF of 10 and 10? _____

8. Jack has 12 balloons and 18 stickers. He wants to put them in envelopes with the same number of balloons and the same number of stickers in each envelope.

a) Jack puts all the balloons and stickers in 2 envelopes.

i) How many balloons would be in each envelope? _____

ii) How many stickers would be in each envelope? _____

b) Can Jack have 4 envelopes with the same number of stickers in each envelope? _____

Why? _____

c) Complete the table to find the different ways Jack can put balloons and stickers in envelopes.

d) What is the relationship between the number of envelopes and the numbers 12 and 18?

Number of Envelopes	Number of Balloons in Each Envelope	Number of Stickers in Each Envelope
1	12	18
2		

NS6-22 Divisibility by 2, 3, 5, and 9

These statements all mean the same thing:

8 is a multiple of 2   2 is a factor of 8   8 is divisible by 2   8 has 2 as a factor

1. a) Shade the numbers that have 2 as a factor.

    b) What are the ones digits of the numbers you shaded in the third row?

    _____

    c) What are the ones digits of the numbers you shaded in *any* row?

    _____

    d) How can you tell whether a number has 2 as a factor without counting up?

    _____

    _____

1	2	3	4	5	6	7	8	9	10
11	12	13	14	15	16	17	18	19	20
21	22	23	24	25	26	27	28	29	30
31	32	33	34	35	36	37	38	39	40
41	42	43	44	45	46	47	48	49	50
51	52	53	54	55	56	57	58	59	60
61	62	63	64	65	66	67	68	69	70
71	72	73	74	75	76	77	78	79	80
81	82	83	84	85	86	87	88	89	90
91	92	93	94	95	96	97	98	99	100

2. a) Shade the numbers that have 5 as a factor.

    b) What are the ones digits of the numbers you shaded in the third row?

    _____

    c) What are the ones digits of the numbers you shaded in *any* row?

    _____

    d) How can you tell whether a number has 5 as a factor without counting up?

    _____

    _____

1	2	3	4	5	6	7	8	9	10
11	12	13	14	15	16	17	18	19	20
21	22	23	24	25	26	27	28	29	30
31	32	33	34	35	36	37	38	39	40
41	42	43	44	45	46	47	48	49	50
51	52	53	54	55	56	57	58	59	60
61	62	63	64	65	66	67	68	69	70
71	72	73	74	75	76	77	78	79	80
81	82	83	84	85	86	87	88	89	90
91	92	93	94	95	96	97	98	99	100

3. Circle the numbers that are divisible by 2.

    9   26   35   78   197   236   1870   4005   23 463

4. Circle the numbers that are divisible by 5.

    10   17   45   52   300   805   4986   7860   35 904

5. Underline the numbers in Question 4 that are divisible by both 2 and 5.

BONUS ▶ What two-digit number is a factor of the numbers you underlined? _____

6.

a) Shade the numbers that are multiples of 9.

b) What number do you get if you add up the digits of the number you shaded in the third row? _____

c) Do you get a multiple of 9 when you add the digits? _____

d) What number do you get if you add up the digits of the number you shaded in the last row? _____

e) Do you get a multiple of 9 when you add the digits? _____

f) How can you tell whether a number is divisible by 9 without counting up? _____

1	2	3	4	5	6	7	8	9	10
11	12	13	14	15	16	17	18	19	20
21	22	23	24	25	26	27	28	29	30
31	32	33	34	35	36	37	38	39	40
41	42	43	44	45	46	47	48	49	50
51	52	53	54	55	56	57	58	59	60
61	62	63	64	65	66	67	68	69	70
71	72	73	74	75	76	77	78	79	80
81	82	83	84	85	86	87	88	89	90
91	92	93	94	95	96	97	98	99	100

7.

a) Shade the numbers that are multiples of 3.

b) What numbers do you get if you add up the digits of the numbers you shaded in the second row? _____ , _____ , _____

c) Do you get multiples of 3 when you add the digits? _____

d) What numbers do you get if you add up the digits of the numbers you shaded in the last row? _____ , _____ , _____

e) Do you get multiples of 3 when you add the digits? _____

f) How can you tell whether a number is divisible by 3 without counting up? _____

1	2	3	4	5	6	7	8	9	10
11	12	13	14	15	16	17	18	19	20
21	22	23	24	25	26	27	28	29	30
31	32	33	34	35	36	37	38	39	40
41	42	43	44	45	46	47	48	49	50
51	52	53	54	55	56	57	58	59	60
61	62	63	64	65	66	67	68	69	70
71	72	73	74	75	76	77	78	79	80
81	82	83	84	85	86	87	88	89	90
91	92	93	94	95	96	97	98	99	100

8.

a) Find the sum of the digits for each number in the table below.

Number	23	33	45	57	68	77	81	95	99	132
Sum of Digits	5	6								

b) Sort the numbers into the Venn diagram.

c) Which region of the Venn diagram is empty?

_____

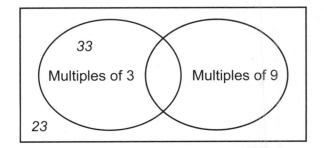

9. Circle the numbers that are divisible by 9.

9   46   55   72   197   213   3870   5004   11 346

10. Circle the numbers that are divisible by 3.

10   15   45   52   300   525   3721   8730   42 125

11. In Question 10, underline the numbers that are divisible by both 3 and 9.

BONUS ▶ Is it possible for a number to be divisible by 9 but not by 3? Why?

_____

_____

12. a) Sort the whole numbers from 0 to 30 into the Venn diagram below.

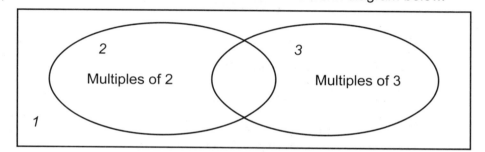

b) In the Venn diagram, where are the numbers that are divisible by 6? _____

Why did that happen? _____

c) Use the tests for divisibility by 2 and 3 to make a test for divisibility by 6. _____

_____

d) Circle the multiples of 6.   72   88   941   642   153   2340   4500   6903

13. Find and list all the factors of the number using a divisibility test or long division in your notebook.

a) 35 _1, 5, 7, 35_ _____   b) 18 _____

c) 28 _____   d) 48 _____

e) 54 _____   f) 76 _____

14. Ava has 174 marbles and she wants to divide the marbles into smaller groups with none left over. Ava wants to put the same number of marbles in each bag. Circle the number of bags that Ava can use.

2 bags   3 bags   5 bags   6 bags   9 bags

NS6-23 Prime Numbers and Composite Numbers

1. List the factors of each number.

Number	Factors
2	1, 2
3	1, 3
4	1, 2, 4
5	
6	
7	
8	
9	
10	

Number	Factors
11	
12	
13	
14	
15	
16	
17	
18	
19	

2. The numbers greater than 1 are either **prime** or **composite**, but never both.

Prime	Composite
2, 3, 5, 7, 11, 13, 17, 19	4, 6, 8, 9, 10, 12, 14, 15, 16, 18

   a) Circle the prime numbers in Question 1.

   b) How many factors does each prime number have? _____

> A whole number is called **prime** if it has exactly two factors. A whole number is called **composite** if it has more than two factors.

3. a) How many factors does the number 1 have? _____

   b) Is the number 1 prime, composite, or neither? _____

4. a) Circle the prime numbers.

   1   22   13   45   75   16   72   81   17   19   99

   b) Is it faster to show that a prime number is prime or that a composite number is composite? Explain.

   _____

   _____

REMINDER ▶ Any whole number is a multiple of each of its factors.

Example: $2 \times 3 = 6$, so 6 is a multiple of 2 and 6 is a multiple of 3.

5. Write "multiple" or "factor."

a) 10 is a _____ of 2 and 2 is a _____ of 10.

b) 10 is a _____ of 20 and 20 is a _____ of 10.

6. Skip count to check for a multiple.   *Skip counting:*

a) Is 36 a multiple of 8? _____

_____, _____, _____, _____, _____

b) Is 42 a multiple of 9? _____

_____, _____, _____, _____, _____

c) Is 35 a multiple of 7? _____

_____, _____, _____, _____, _____

d) Is 24 a multiple of 6? _____

_____, _____, _____, _____, _____

7. Use long division to decide if the number is a multiple of 4.

a)

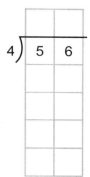

Is 56 a multiple of 4? _____

b)

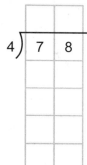

Is 78 a multiple of 4? _____

c)

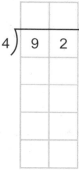

Is 92 a multiple of 4? _____

REMINDER ▶ An even number is a multiple of 2. So all even numbers have 2 as a factor.

8. a) Finish writing the factor pair of the number.

i) 6

2 and _____

ii) 20

2 and _____

iii) 64

2 and _____

BONUS ▶ 48 426

2 and _____

b) Which even numbers are composite? Explain. _____

_____

_____

Anna creates a **factor tree** to find prime factors of 20.

Step 1
Anna finds any pair of numbers (not including 1) that multiply to give 20 and shades the prime numbers.

Step 2
Anna repeats Step 1 for the numbers on the "branches" that are not prime numbers.

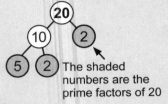

The shaded numbers are the prime factors of 20

Anna stops when all numbers on the branches are prime numbers and shaded.

9. Complete the factor tree for the number. (Remember to shade any prime numbers.)

a)
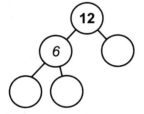

b)
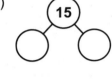

c)
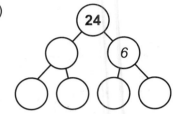

The **prime factorization** of a composite number means writing the number as a product of prime numbers.

Examples: The prime factorization of 6 is 2 × 3. The prime factorization of 20 is 5 × 2 × 2.

10. Write the prime factorization of each number in Question 9.

a) 12 = _____ × _____ × _____

b) 15 = _____ × _____

c) 24 = _____ × _____ × _____ × _____

11. Use a factor tree to find the prime factorization.

a)
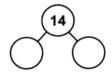

14 = _____ × _____

b)
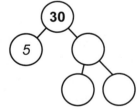

30 = _____ × _____ × _____

c)
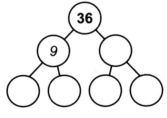

36 = _____ × _____ × _____ × _____

d) 16   e) 18   f) 48

12. a) Complete the two factor trees for 28.

    b) Write the prime factorization for each tree.

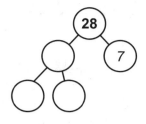 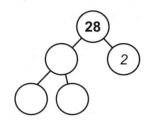

       Left tree: _____ × _____ × _____

       Right tree: _____ × _____ × _____

    c) If you write the prime factors from least to greatest,
do you see any differences between the factorizations? _____

13. a) Complete the two factor trees for 40.

    b) Write the prime factors from least to greatest
for each tree to show that the prime
factorizations are the same

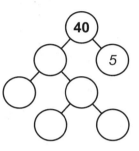 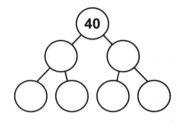

       Left tree: _____ × _____ × _____ × _____

       Right tree: _____ × _____ × _____ × _____

    BONUS ▶ Complete the factor tree for 40 with the same shape as the left tree in
part a) but with different numbers. Does the third tree give the same
prime factorization?

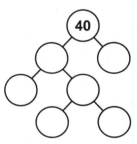

14. Write five odd multiples of 3 between 10 and 40: _____, _____, _____, _____, _____

15. I am a prime number less than 10. If you add either 10 or 30 to me, the result is a
prime number. What number am I? _____

16. Ren has 12 roses and 16 lilies. He wants to use all his flowers to make bouquets.
Each bouquet must have the same number of roses and the same number of lilies.
What is the greatest number of bouquets that he can make?

BONUS ▶ Megan has 12 apples, 18 oranges, and 30 bananas. She wants to put all
the fruits into baskets so that each basket has the same number of each fruit.
Megan uses the greatest number of baskets as she can. How many of each
type of fruit are in each basket?

NS6-24 Order of Operations

1. a) Add the same numbers two ways. Do the addition in brackets first.

i) $(4 + 6) + 5$ $4 + (6 + 5)$ ii) $(3 + 7) + 2$ $3 + (7 + 2)$

     $= \underline{\hspace{1cm}} + 5$ $= 4 + \underline{\hspace{1cm}}$ $= \underline{\hspace{1cm}} + \underline{\hspace{1cm}}$ $= \underline{\hspace{1cm}} + \underline{\hspace{1cm}}$

     $= \underline{\hspace{1cm}}$ $= \underline{\hspace{1cm}}$ $= \underline{\hspace{1cm}}$ $= \underline{\hspace{1cm}}$

b) Does the answer change depending on which addition you do first? _____

2. a) Subtract the same numbers two ways. Do the subtraction in brackets first.

i) $(7 - 4) - 2$ $7 - (4 - 2)$ ii) $10 - (4 - 3)$ $(10 - 4) - 3$

     $= \underline{\hspace{1cm}} - \underline{\hspace{1cm}}$ $= \underline{\hspace{1cm}} - \underline{\hspace{1cm}}$ $= \underline{\hspace{1cm}} - \underline{\hspace{1cm}}$ $= \underline{\hspace{1cm}} - \underline{\hspace{1cm}}$

     $= \underline{\hspace{1cm}}$ $= \underline{\hspace{1cm}}$ $= \underline{\hspace{1cm}}$ $= \underline{\hspace{1cm}}$

b) Does the answer change depending on which subtraction you do first? _____

> Add and subtract in the order you read: from left to right.

3. Add or subtract from left to right.

a) $7 + 3 - 2$ b) $7 - 3 + 2$ c) $8 + 4 + 2$ d) $10 - 4 - 3$

   $= \underline{\;\;10 - 2\;\;}$ $= \underline{\hspace{1.5cm}}$ $= \underline{\hspace{1.5cm}}$ $= \underline{\hspace{1.5cm}}$

   $= \underline{\;\;8\;\;}$ $= \underline{\hspace{1cm}}$ $= \underline{\hspace{1cm}}$ $= \underline{\hspace{1cm}}$

> Multiplication and division are also done from left to right.

4. Multiply or divide from left to right.

a) $4 \times 3 \div 6$ b) $8 \div 2 \times 5$ c) $10 \times 2 \times 3$ d) $24 \div 2 \div 3$

   $= \underline{\hspace{1.5cm}}$ $= \underline{\hspace{1.5cm}}$ $= \underline{\hspace{1.5cm}}$ $= \underline{\hspace{1.5cm}}$

   $= \underline{\hspace{1cm}}$ $= \underline{\hspace{1cm}}$ $= \underline{\hspace{1cm}}$ $= \underline{\hspace{1cm}}$

> When evaluating expressions, first do all multiplications and divisions from left to right.
> Then do all additions and subtractions from left to right.

5. Circle the operation you would do first.

a) $3 + \boxed{4 \times 2}$ b) $10 - 3 + 4$ c) $8 + 2 \div 2$ d) $12 - 6 \div 3$

e) $8 \div 4 \times 3$ f) $8 - 2 \times 3$ g) $7 + 3 - 4$ h) $8 \times 3 - 4$

i) $15 \div 3 + 2$ j) $12 \div 6 - 2$ k) $5 \times 4 + 3$ l) $5 \times 4 \div 2$

6. Which operation is done first? Do it, then rewrite the rest of the expression.

a) $7 + 4 - 3$

$= \underline{\quad 11 - 3 \quad}$

b) $6 + 4 \div 2$

$= \underline{\quad 6 + 2 \quad}$

c) $10 \div 2 + 3$

$= \underline{\qquad\qquad}$

d) $12 \div 3 \times 2$

$= \underline{\qquad\qquad}$

e) $12 - 7 - 4$

$= \underline{\qquad\qquad}$

f) $3 \times 4 \div 2$

$= \underline{\qquad\qquad}$

g) $8 \div 4 - 2$

$= \underline{\qquad\qquad}$

h) $8 - 3 + 2$

$= \underline{\qquad\qquad}$

i) $3 \times 20 \div 10$

$= \underline{\qquad\qquad}$

> If there are brackets in an expression, do the operations in brackets first.
> Example: $7 - 3 + 2 = 4 + 2$ but $7 - (3 + 2) = 7 - 5$
> $\qquad\qquad\qquad\quad = 6 \qquad\qquad\qquad\qquad\qquad = 2$

7. Do the operation in brackets first. Then write the answer.

a) $10 + (4 \times 2)$

$= \underline{\quad 10 + 8 \quad}$

$= \underline{\quad 18 \quad}$

b) $(10 + 4) \times 2$

$= \underline{\qquad\qquad}$

$= \underline{\qquad}$

c) $(10 + 4) \div 2$

$= \underline{\qquad\qquad}$

$= \underline{\qquad}$

d) $10 + (4 \div 2)$

$= \underline{\qquad\qquad}$

$= \underline{\qquad}$

e) $10 - (4 \times 2)$

$= \underline{\qquad\qquad}$

$= \underline{\qquad}$

f) $(10 - 4) \times 2$

$= \underline{\qquad\qquad}$

$= \underline{\qquad}$

g) $(10 - 4) \div 2$

h) $10 - (4 \div 2)$

i) $12 \times (3 \times 2)$

j) $(12 \times 3) \times 2$

k) $(8 \div 4) \div 2$

l) $8 \div (4 \div 2)$

> To avoid writing brackets all the time, mathematicians use a standard **order of operations**:
> 1. Do operations in brackets.
> 2. Do all multiplications and divisions from left to right.
> 3. Do all additions and subtractions from left to right.

8. Do the operations one at a time, in the standard order.

a) $10 \div 2 \times (5 - 2)$

$= \underline{\quad 10 \div 2 \times 3 \quad}$

$= \underline{\quad 5 \times 3 \quad}$

$= \underline{\quad 15 \quad}$

b) $(9 + 12) \div 3 \times 2$

$= \underline{\qquad\qquad\qquad}$

$= \underline{\qquad\qquad\qquad}$

$= \underline{\qquad}$

c) $(13 - 3) \div (7 - 2)$

$= \underline{\qquad\qquad\qquad}$

$= \underline{\qquad\qquad\qquad}$

$= \underline{\qquad}$

NS6-25 Naming Fractions and Models of Fractions

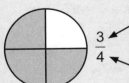

The pie is cut into 4 equal parts.

3 parts out of 4 are shaded.

$\frac{3}{4}$ of the pie is shaded.

$\frac{3}{4}$ ← The **numerator** (3) tells you how many parts are shaded.

← The **denominator** (4) tells you how many equal parts are in a whole.

1. Name the fraction.

a) $\frac{3}{8}$

b)

c)

d)

e)

f)

g)

h)

2. Shade the given fraction.

a) $\frac{3}{6}$

b) $\frac{2}{5}$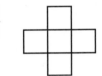

c) $\frac{5}{9}$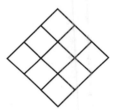

3. Use one of the following words to describe the parts in the models below.

halves   thirds   fourths   fifths   sixths   sevenths   eighths   ninths

a)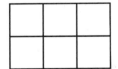

_____sixths_____

b)

_____

c)

_____

d)

_____

e)

_____

f)

_____

4. Sketch a circle cut into …

a) thirds

b) quarters (or fourths)

c) eighths

5. Use a centimetre ruler to divide the line segment into the given number of equal parts.

   a) 5 equal parts   b) 3 equal parts   c) 4 equal parts

   d) 7 equal parts   e) 8 equal parts

6. Use a centimetre ruler to divide the box into the given number of equal parts.

   a) 4 equal parts   b) 5 equal parts

   c) 3 equal parts   d) 6 equal parts

7. Using a centimetre ruler, find what fraction of the box is shaded.

   a)   b)

      is shaded   is shaded

   c)   d)

      is shaded   is shaded

8. Using a centimetre ruler, complete the figure to make a whole.

   a) $\dfrac{1}{2}$ b) $\dfrac{1}{3}$ c) $\dfrac{1}{4}$

9. You have $\dfrac{3}{5}$ of a pie.

   a) What does the bottom (denominator) of the fraction tell you?

   b) What does the top (numerator) of the fraction tell you?

10. Explain why the picture does (or does not) show $\dfrac{1}{4}$.

    a)   b)   c)   BONUS ▶

NS6-26 Equal Parts of a Set

Fractions can name or describe parts of a set. Example:

$\frac{3}{5}$ of the shapes are triangles, $\frac{1}{5}$ are squares, $\frac{1}{5}$ are circles.

1. Complete the sentence.

a) $\frac{4}{7}$ of the shapes are _____.

b) $\frac{2}{7}$ of the shapes are _____.

c) $\frac{1}{7}$ of the shapes are _____.

d) $\frac{3}{7}$ of the shapes are _____.

2. Complete the sentences.

a)

[ ] of the shapes are triangles.

[ ] of the shapes are shaded.

b)

[ ] of the shapes are squares.

[ ] of the shapes are shaded.

3. Describe the picture in two different ways using the fraction $\frac{3}{5}$.

_____

_____

4. A football team wins 7 games and loses 5 games.

a) How many games did the team play? _____

b) What fraction of the games did the team win? [ ]

c) What fraction of the games did the team lose? [ ]

d) Did the team win more than half its games? _____

5. Answer the question using the information in the table.

a) What fraction of the students in each class have siblings?

Class A [ ]   Class B [ ]

	Has Siblings	Has No Siblings
Class A	2	3
Class B	1	2

b) What fraction of all the students have siblings? [ ]

6. What fraction of the letters in the word "Alberta" are …

a) vowels? [ ]

b) consonants? [ ]

7. Express 11 months as a fraction of one year. [ ]

8.

△ ◼ ◻ ○ ○ ▨ ◻ ◻ ◍

a) [ ] of the shapes are circles.

b) [ ] of the shapes are triangles.

c) [ ] of the shapes are striped.

d) [ ] of the shapes are white.

9. Write two more fraction statements for the figures in Question 8.

[ ] of the shapes are _____.

[ ] of the shapes are _____.

10. Draw the shaded and unshaded shapes and then answer the question.

a) There are 7 circles and squares.

$\frac{2}{7}$ of the shapes are squares.

$\frac{5}{7}$ of the shapes are shaded.

3 circles are shaded.

How many squares are shaded?

b) There are 8 triangles and squares.

$\frac{3}{8}$ of the shapes are shaded.

$\frac{2}{8}$ of the shapes are triangles.

1 triangle is shaded.

How many squares are not shaded?

NS6-27 Introduction to Adding and Subtracting Fractions

1. Imagine moving the shaded pieces from pies A and B onto pie plate C. Show how much of pie plate C would be filled and then write a fraction for pie C.

   A. 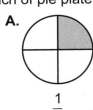   **B.**   **C.**

   $\dfrac{1}{4}$ $+$ $\dfrac{2}{4}$ $=$

2. Imagine pouring the liquid from the two cups into the empty cup. Shade the amount of liquid that would be in the empty cup. Then complete the addition sentence.

   a)

   $\dfrac{3}{5}$ $+$ $\dfrac{}{5}$ $=$ $\dfrac{}{}$

   b)

   $\dfrac{}{3}$ $+$ $\dfrac{}{3}$ $=$ $\dfrac{}{}$

3. Add.

   a) $\dfrac{2}{5} + \dfrac{1}{5} =$ b) $\dfrac{1}{4} + \dfrac{1}{4} =$ c) $\dfrac{4}{7} + \dfrac{2}{7} =$ d) $\dfrac{4}{9} + \dfrac{1}{9} =$

   e) $\dfrac{5}{13} + \dfrac{6}{13} =$ f) $\dfrac{7}{23} + \dfrac{11}{23} =$ g) $\dfrac{8}{25} + \dfrac{13}{25} =$ h) $\dfrac{19}{43} + \dfrac{18}{43} =$

4. Show how much pie would be left if you took away the amount shown. Then complete the subtraction sentence.

   a)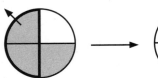

   $\dfrac{3}{4} - \dfrac{2}{4}$ $=$ $\dfrac{}{}$

   b)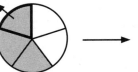

   $\dfrac{3}{5} - \dfrac{1}{5}$ $=$ $\dfrac{}{}$

5. Subtract.

   a) $\dfrac{4}{7} - \dfrac{1}{7} =$ b) $\dfrac{2}{5} - \dfrac{1}{5} =$ c) $\dfrac{2}{3} - \dfrac{1}{3} =$ d) $\dfrac{7}{8} - \dfrac{5}{8} =$

   e) $\dfrac{11}{13} - \dfrac{10}{13} =$ f) $\dfrac{7}{18} - \dfrac{2}{18} =$ g) $\dfrac{23}{27} - \dfrac{16}{27} =$ h) $\dfrac{31}{73} - \dfrac{11}{73} =$

NS6-28 Comparing and Ordering Fractions

1. What fraction has a greater numerator, $\frac{2}{6}$ or $\frac{5}{6}$?

   Which fraction is greater?

   Explain your thinking. _____

   _____

2. Circle the greater fraction in the pair.

   a) $\frac{6}{16}$ or $\frac{9}{16}$ b) $\frac{5}{8}$ or $\frac{3}{8}$ c) $\frac{24}{25}$ or $\frac{22}{25}$ d) $\frac{37}{53}$ or $\frac{27}{53}$

3. Two fractions have the same denominators (bottoms) but different numerators (tops). How can you tell which fraction is greater?

   _____

   _____

4. Circle the greater fraction in the pair.

   a) $\frac{1}{8}$ or $\frac{1}{9}$ b) $\frac{12}{12}$ or $\frac{12}{13}$ c) $\frac{5}{225}$ or $\frac{5}{125}$ d) $\frac{61}{253}$ or $\frac{61}{514}$

5. Fraction A and Fraction B have the same numerators but different denominators. How can you tell which fraction is greater?

   _____

   _____

6. Circle the greater fraction in the pair.

   a) $\frac{2}{3}$ or $\frac{2}{9}$ b) $\frac{7}{17}$ or $\frac{11}{17}$ c) $\frac{6}{288}$ or $\frac{6}{18}$ d) $\frac{93}{174}$ or $\frac{74}{174}$

7. Write the fractions in order from least to greatest.

   a) $\frac{2}{3}, \frac{1}{3}, \frac{3}{3}$ ☐ < ☐ < ☐   b) $\frac{9}{10}, \frac{2}{10}, \frac{1}{10}, \frac{5}{10}$ ☐ < ☐ < ☐ < ☐

   c) $\frac{1}{7}, \frac{1}{3}, \frac{1}{13}$ ☐ < ☐ < ☐   d) $\frac{2}{11}, \frac{2}{5}, \frac{2}{7}, \frac{2}{16}$ ☐ < ☐ < ☐ < ☐

8. Which fraction is greater, $\frac{1}{2}$ or $\frac{45}{100}$? Explain your thinking.

9. Is it possible for $\frac{1}{4}$ of a pie to be bigger than $\frac{1}{2}$ of another pie? Show your thinking with a picture.

Matt and his friends ate the amount of pie shown.

They ate three and one quarter pies altogether (or $3\frac{1}{4}$ pies).

3 whole pies   and $\frac{1}{4}$ of another pie

$3\frac{1}{4}$ is called a **mixed number** because it is a mixture of a whole number and a fraction.

1. Write how many whole pies are shaded.

a)

b)

c)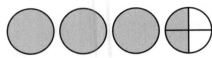

___2___ whole pies   _____ whole pie   _____ whole pies

2. Write the shaded area as a mixed number.

a)  $2\frac{1}{4}$ ____

b) 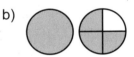 ____

c)  ____

d)  ____

e) 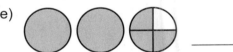 ____

f)  ____

g)  ____

3. Shade the amount of pie given in the mixed number. There may be more pies than you need.

a) $3\frac{1}{2}$

b) $1\frac{1}{4}$

c) $2\frac{3}{4}$

d) $3\frac{2}{3}$

e) $1\frac{2}{5}$

f) $2\frac{5}{6}$

4. Sketch pies for the mixed number.

a) $2\frac{1}{3}$ pies   b) $3\frac{3}{4}$ pies   c) $2\frac{3}{5}$ pies   d) $4\frac{1}{2}$ pies

Ava and her friends ate 9 quarter-sized pieces of pizza.

Altogether they ate $\frac{9}{4}$ pizzas.

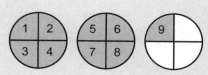

When the numerator of a fraction is larger than the denominator, the fraction represents more than a whole. Such fractions are called **improper fractions**.

5. Describe the shaded area as an improper fraction.

a) 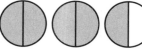 $\frac{5}{2}$

b)  ____

c)  ____

d)  ____

e) 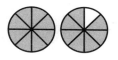 ____

f)  ____

g) 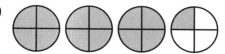 ____

h) 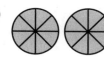 ____

6. Shade one piece at a time until you have shaded the improper fraction.

a) $\frac{5}{2}$

b) $\frac{7}{4}$

c) $\frac{11}{3}$

d) $\frac{12}{4}$

e) $\frac{17}{5}$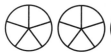

f) $\frac{21}{8}$

g) $\frac{17}{6}$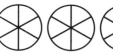

h) $\frac{11}{5}$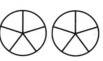

7. Sketch pies for the improper fraction.

a) $\frac{6}{4}$ pies

b) $\frac{7}{2}$ pies

c) $\frac{11}{4}$ pies

d) $\frac{13}{3}$ pies

8. Is the fraction more than a whole? How do you know?

a) $\frac{9}{10}$

b) $\frac{15}{7}$

c) $\frac{12}{8}$

NS6-30 Mixed Numbers and Improper Fractions

How many quarter pieces are in $2\frac{3}{4}$ pies?

4 quarters   8 (= 2 × 4) quarters   8 quarters + 3 extra quarters = 11 quarters

So there are 11 quarters altogether in $2\frac{3}{4}$ pies.

1. Find the number of halves in the amount.

   a) 1 pie = _____ halves

   b) 2 pies = _____ halves

   c) 3 pies = _____ halves

   d) $2\frac{1}{2}$ pies = _____ halves

   e) $3\frac{1}{2}$ pies = _____ halves

   f) $4\frac{1}{2}$ pies = _____ halves

2. Find the number of thirds or quarters in the amount.

   a) 1 pie = _____ thirds

   b) 2 pies = _____ thirds

   c) 3 pies = _____ thirds

   d) $1\frac{2}{3}$ pies = _____ thirds

   e) $2\frac{1}{3}$ pies = _____ thirds

   f) $4\frac{2}{3}$ pies = _____ thirds

   g) 1 pie = _____ quarters

   h) 2 pies = _____ quarters

   i) 5 pies = _____ quarters

   j) $2\frac{3}{4}$ pies = _____ quarters

   k) $5\frac{1}{4}$ pies = _____ quarters

   l) $5\frac{3}{4}$ pies = _____ quarters

3. If 1 box holds 4 cans, then …

   a) 2 boxes hold _____ cans.

   b) 3 boxes hold _____ cans.

   c) 4 boxes hold _____ cans.

   d) $2\frac{1}{4}$ boxes hold _____ cans.

   e) $3\frac{1}{4}$ boxes hold _____ cans.

   f) $4\frac{3}{4}$ boxes hold _____ cans.

4. If 1 box holds 6 cans, then …

   a) $2\frac{1}{6}$ boxes hold _____ cans.

   b) $2\frac{5}{6}$ boxes hold _____ cans.

   c) $3\frac{1}{6}$ boxes hold _____ cans.

5. Pens come in packs of 6. Peter used $1\frac{5}{6}$ packs. How many pens did he use? _____

6. Ella needs $4\frac{2}{3}$ cups of flour.

   a) Which scoop should she use? _____

   b) How many scoops will she need? _____

   A $\frac{1}{3}$ cup

   B $\frac{1}{4}$ cup

How many whole pies are there in $\frac{13}{4}$ pies?

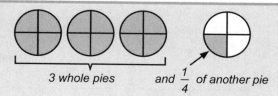

There are 13 pieces altogether and each pie has 4 pieces.

So you can find the number of whole pies by dividing 13 by 4: $13 \div 4 = 3$ Remainder 1

There are 3 whole pies and 1 quarter left over, so: $\frac{13}{4} = 3\frac{1}{4}$

3 whole pies   and $\frac{1}{4}$ of another pie

7. Find the number of whole pies in the amount by dividing.

a) $\frac{6}{2}$ pies = _____ whole pies   b) $\frac{15}{3}$ pies = _____ whole pies   c) $\frac{16}{4}$ pies = _____ whole pies

8. Find the number of whole pies and the number of pieces remaining by dividing.

a) $\frac{7}{2}$ pies = ___3___ whole pies and ___1___ half pie = $3\frac{1}{2}$ pies

b) $\frac{11}{3}$ pies = _____ whole pies and _____ thirds = _____ pies

c) $\frac{15}{4}$ pies = _____ whole pies and _____ = _____ pies

9. a) Write a mixed number and an improper fraction for the number of litres.

Mixed number: Improper fraction:

b) Write a mixed number and an improper fraction for the length of the rope.

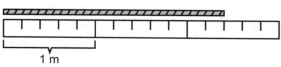

Mixed number: Improper fraction:

10. Write the improper fraction as a mixed number by dividing.

a) $\frac{9}{2}$

$9 \div 2 =$ _____ R _____

So $\frac{9}{2} =$

b) $\frac{15}{4}$

$15 \div 4 =$ _____ R _____

So $\frac{15}{4} =$

c) $\frac{22}{5}$

$22 \div 5 =$ _____ R _____

So $\frac{22}{5} =$

d) $\frac{14}{5} =$ e) $\frac{68}{10} =$ f) $\frac{32}{3} =$ g) $\frac{28}{7} =$ h) $\frac{40}{7} =$ i) $\frac{30}{8} =$

11. Draw a picture to find out which number is greater.

a) $3\frac{1}{2}$ or $\frac{5}{2}$ b) $2\frac{4}{5}$ or $\frac{12}{5}$ c) $4\frac{1}{3}$ or $\frac{14}{3}$

NS6-31 Comparing Fractions on a Number Line

1. Use the number line to complete the chart.

	$\frac{0}{5}$	$\frac{1}{5}$	$\frac{2}{5}$	$\frac{3}{5}$	$\frac{4}{5}$	$\frac{5}{5}$	$\frac{6}{5}$	$\frac{7}{5}$	$\frac{8}{5}$	$\frac{9}{5}$	$\frac{10}{5}$
	0	$\frac{1}{5}$	$\frac{2}{5}$	$\frac{3}{5}$	$\frac{4}{5}$	1	$1\frac{1}{5}$	$1\frac{2}{5}$	$1\frac{3}{5}$	$1\frac{4}{5}$	2

Mixed Number	$1\frac{4}{5}$			$1\frac{1}{5}$		
Improper Fraction		$\frac{7}{5}$	$\frac{10}{5}$		$\frac{8}{5}$	$\frac{5}{5}$

2. Fill in the number line, then compare the mixed number to the improper fraction. Write $<$, $>$, or $=$ in the box.

a)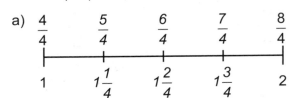

$1\frac{3}{4} \boxed{>} \frac{5}{4}$

b)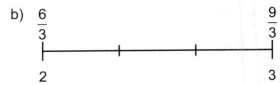

$2\frac{1}{3} \boxed{} \frac{8}{3}$

c)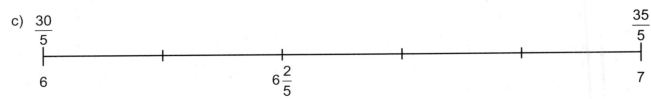

i) $6\frac{2}{5} \boxed{} \frac{34}{5}$ ii) $6\frac{3}{5} \boxed{} \frac{30}{5}$ iii) $6\frac{1}{5} \boxed{} \frac{31}{5}$ iv) $6\frac{4}{5} \boxed{} \frac{35}{5}$

d)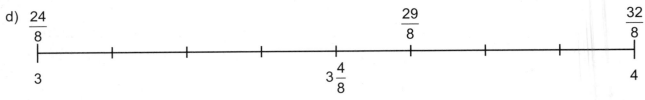

i) $3\frac{7}{8} \boxed{} \frac{29}{8}$ ii) $3\frac{3}{8} \boxed{} \frac{27}{8}$ iii) $3\frac{5}{8} \boxed{} \frac{27}{8}$ iv) $4 \boxed{} \frac{32}{8}$

3. What two whole numbers is $\frac{32}{9}$ between? Draw a number line to show your answer.

4. Don's party guests ate $\frac{34}{6}$ pies. Don had less than 1 pie left over. How many pies did he bake?

NS6-32 Equivalent Fractions and Multiplication

1. Compare the pair of circles.

a) has ___three___ times as many parts as

b) has _____ times as many parts as

c) has _____ times as many parts as

d) has _____ times as many parts as

2. Fill in the blanks.

a) A has ___two___ times as many parts as B.

A has _____ times as many shaded parts as B.

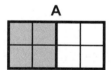

b) A has _____ times as many parts as B.

A has _____ times as many shaded parts as B.

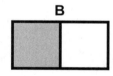

c) A has _____ times as many parts as B.

A has _____ times as many shaded parts as B.

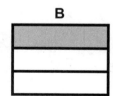

d) A has _____ times as many parts as B.

A has _____ times as many shaded parts as B.

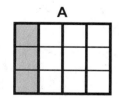

Equivalent fractions are fractions that have the same value or represent the same amount.

3. Write an equivalent fraction for the picture. Then write how many times the numerator and denominator are multiplied.

a)
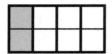

$$\frac{1}{4} \xrightarrow[\times 2]{\times 2} = \frac{2}{8}$$

equivalent fractions

b)

$$\frac{1}{3} \xrightarrow[\times]{\times} = \frac{\square}{\square}$$

c)
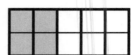

$$\frac{2}{5} \xrightarrow[\times]{\times} = \frac{\square}{\square}$$

d)
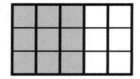

$$\frac{3}{5} \xrightarrow[\times 3]{\times 3} = \frac{\square}{\square}$$

e)
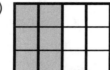

$$\frac{2}{4} \xrightarrow[\times]{\times} = \frac{\square}{\square}$$

f)

$$\frac{2}{3} \xrightarrow[\times]{\times} = \frac{\square}{\square}$$

g)
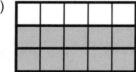

$$\frac{2}{3} \xrightarrow[\times]{\times} = \frac{\square}{\square}$$

h)
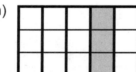

$$\frac{1}{5} \xrightarrow[\times]{\times} = \frac{\square}{\square}$$

i)
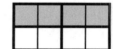

$$\frac{2}{4} \xrightarrow[\times]{\times} = \frac{\square}{\square}$$

BONUS ▶ Write two fractions to describe the shaded portion.

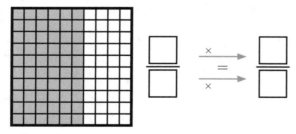

$$\frac{\square}{\square} \xrightarrow[\times]{\times} = \frac{\square}{\square}$$

4. Draw a picture to show that $\frac{3}{4}$ and $\frac{6}{8}$ are equivalent.

You can multiply the numerator and denominator by the same number to get an equivalent fraction.

Example: Picture A   Picture B

$$\frac{3}{4} \xrightarrow[\times 2]{\times 2} \frac{6}{8}$$

Picture B has twice as many **parts** as Picture A.
Picture B has twice as many **shaded parts** as Picture A.

5. Draw lines to cut the pies into more pieces. Then fill in the numerators of the equivalent fractions.

a)

4 pieces   6 pieces   8 pieces

$$\frac{1}{2} = \frac{}{4} = \frac{}{6} = \frac{}{8}$$

b)

6 pieces   9 pieces   12 pieces

$$\frac{1}{3} = \frac{}{6} = \frac{}{9} = \frac{}{12}$$

6. Cut the pie into more pieces. Then fill in the missing numbers.

a)
$$\frac{1}{3} \xrightarrow[\times 2]{\times 2} \frac{}{6}$$

↑ *This number tells you how many pieces to cut each slice into.*

b)
$$\frac{2}{4} \xrightarrow[\times 2]{\times 2} \frac{}{8}$$

c)
$$\frac{2}{3} \xrightarrow[\times]{\times} \frac{}{9}$$

7. Use multiplication to find the equivalent fraction or equivalent improper fraction.

a) $\frac{2}{3} \xrightarrow[\times 2]{\times 2} \frac{}{6}$

b) $\frac{1}{2} = \frac{}{10}$

c) $\frac{3}{2} = \frac{}{10}$

d) $\frac{1}{4} = \frac{}{12}$

e) $\frac{7}{4} = \frac{}{16}$

f) $\frac{3}{5} = \frac{18}{}$

g) $\frac{11}{5} = \frac{}{20}$

h) $\frac{9}{4} = \frac{27}{}$

8. a) Write five fractions equivalent to $\frac{2}{3}$.

$$\frac{2}{3} = \boxed{} = \boxed{} = \boxed{} = \boxed{} = \boxed{}$$

b) Write five improper fractions equivalent to $\frac{9}{7}$.

$$\frac{9}{7} = \boxed{} = \boxed{} = \boxed{} = \boxed{} = \boxed{}$$

NS6-33 Comparing Fractions Using Equivalent Fractions

1. Draw lines to cut the pies into more equal pieces. Then fill in the numerators of the equivalent fractions.

   a)

   $$\frac{2}{3} = \frac{}{6} = \frac{}{9} = \frac{}{12}$$

   b)

   $$\frac{3}{4} = \frac{}{8} = \frac{}{12}$$

2. a) Use your answers from Question 1. Write two fractions with the same denominators.

   $$\frac{2}{3} = \boxed{} \text{ and } \frac{3}{4} = \boxed{}$$

   b) Which of the two fractions is greater, $\frac{2}{3}$ or $\frac{3}{4}$? _____

   How do you know? _____

   _____

3. Write equivalent fractions with the same denominator. Then circle the larger fraction.

   a) $\frac{1}{4} = \frac{}{20}$ and $\frac{3}{5} = \frac{}{20}$

   b) $\frac{2}{7} = \frac{}{21}$ and $\frac{2}{3} = \frac{}{21}$

4. a) Write an equivalent fraction with denominator 18.

   i) $\frac{1}{2} = \frac{}{18}$ ii) $\frac{1}{6} = \frac{}{18}$ iii) $\frac{5}{9} = \frac{}{18}$ iv) $\frac{2}{3} = \frac{}{18}$

   b) Write the fractions from part a) in order from least to greatest.

   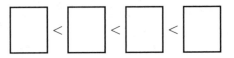

5. Draw lines to cut the left-hand pie into the same number of pieces as the right-hand pie. Complete the equivalent fraction. Then circle the greater fraction.

a)

$$\frac{1}{2} = \qquad \qquad \frac{3}{4}$$

b)

$$\frac{2}{3} = \qquad \qquad \frac{3}{6}$$

To compare $\frac{1}{3}$ and $\frac{2}{5}$ you can change them into fractions with the same denominator.

Multiply the numerator and denominator of the first fraction by the denominator of the second.

Multiply the numerator and denominator of the second fraction by the denominator of the first.

$$\frac{5\times}{5\times}\frac{1}{3} = \frac{5}{15} \qquad \frac{6}{15} = \frac{2}{5}\frac{\times 3}{\times 3}$$

Now the fractions are easy to compare: $\dfrac{5}{15} < \dfrac{6}{15}$, so $\dfrac{1}{3} < \dfrac{2}{5}$

6. Compare the fractions. First, turn the fraction on the left into an equivalent fraction with the same denominator as the fraction on the right. Then write $<$ or $>$ to show which fraction is greater.

a) $\dfrac{2}{3}\dfrac{\times 2}{\times 2} = \dfrac{4}{6} \boxed{<} \dfrac{5}{6}$

b) $\dfrac{3}{4} = \dfrac{}{8} \boxed{} \dfrac{5}{8}$

c) $\dfrac{1}{2} = \dfrac{}{\quad} \boxed{} \dfrac{3}{4}$

d) $\dfrac{1}{2} = \dfrac{}{\quad} \boxed{} \dfrac{4}{10}$

e) $\dfrac{1}{2} = \dfrac{}{\quad} \boxed{} \dfrac{3}{12}$

f) $\dfrac{1}{3} = \dfrac{}{\quad} \boxed{} \dfrac{4}{9}$

g) $\dfrac{5}{6} = \dfrac{}{\quad} \boxed{} \dfrac{13}{18}$

h) $\dfrac{1}{5} = \dfrac{}{\quad} \boxed{} \dfrac{4}{10}$

i) $\dfrac{1}{4} = \dfrac{}{\quad} \boxed{} \dfrac{7}{16}$

7. Turn the fractions into fractions with the same denominator. Then compare with $<$ or $>$.

a) $\dfrac{3\times}{3\times}\dfrac{2}{5} \qquad \dfrac{1}{3}\dfrac{\times 5}{\times 5}$

$= \dfrac{}{15} \qquad = \dfrac{}{15}$

So $\dfrac{2}{5} \boxed{} \dfrac{1}{3}$

b) $\dfrac{3}{4} \qquad \dfrac{2}{3}$

$= \dfrac{}{\quad} \qquad = \dfrac{}{\quad}$

So $\dfrac{3}{4} \boxed{} \dfrac{2}{3}$

c) $\dfrac{1}{2} \qquad \dfrac{2}{5}$

$= \dfrac{}{\quad} \qquad = \dfrac{}{\quad}$

So $\dfrac{1}{2} \boxed{} \dfrac{2}{5}$

d) $\dfrac{2}{3}$ and $\dfrac{5}{8}$

e) $\dfrac{2}{3}$ and $\dfrac{3}{5}$

f) $\dfrac{5}{17}$ and $\dfrac{3}{10}$

8. A turtle weighs $\dfrac{4}{9}$ kg and a lizard weighs $\dfrac{5}{11}$ kg. Which animal is heavier? Explain how you know.

To compare improper fractions $\frac{3}{2}$ and $\frac{6}{5}$, you can change them to have the same denominator.

Multiply the numerator and denominator of $\frac{3}{2}$ by 5.   *Multiply the numerator and denominator of $\frac{6}{5}$ by 2.*

$$\frac{5 \times 3}{5 \times 2} = \frac{15}{10} \qquad \frac{12}{10} = \frac{6 \times 2}{5 \times 2}$$

Now the improper fractions are easy to compare: $\frac{15}{10} > \frac{12}{10}$, so $\frac{3}{2} > \frac{6}{5}$

9. Turn the improper fractions into improper fractions with the same denominator.
Then compare with $<$, $=$, or $>$.

a) $\frac{4 \times 5}{4 \times 3}$ $\frac{7 \times 3}{4 \times 3}$ b) $\frac{5}{2}$ $\frac{7}{3}$ c) $\frac{9}{4}$ $\frac{11}{5}$

   $= \frac{}{12}$ $= \frac{}{12}$ $= \frac{}{}$ $= \frac{}{}$ $= \frac{}{}$ $= \frac{}{}$

   So $\frac{5}{3} \square \frac{7}{4}$ So $\frac{5}{2} \square \frac{7}{3}$ So $\frac{9}{4} \square \frac{11}{5}$

d) $\frac{3}{2}$ and $\frac{9}{6}$ e) $\frac{11}{5}$ and $\frac{7}{3}$ f) $\frac{8}{5}$ and $\frac{10}{7}$

The mixed number with a greater whole number part is greater.

Example: $3\frac{7}{8} < 5\frac{1}{2}$, because $3 < 5$.

To compare mixed numbers with the same whole number part, compare the fraction parts.

Example: $5\frac{3}{7} < 5\frac{3}{4}$, because $\frac{3}{7} < \frac{3}{4}$.

---

10. Compare mixed numbers with $<$, $>$, or $=$. You may need to change the fraction parts
to have the same denominator.

a) $3\frac{3}{4} \square 3\frac{3}{5}$ b) $2\frac{4}{5} \square 3\frac{1}{3}$ c) $4\frac{6}{9} \square 4\frac{2}{3}$

d) $4\frac{2}{3}$ and $4\frac{5}{6}$ e) $7\frac{3}{5}$ and $7\frac{2}{3}$ f) $6\frac{4}{7}$ and $6\frac{1}{2}$

11. Compare by converting improper fractions to mixed numbers.

a) $2\frac{1}{3}$ and $\frac{11}{6}$ b) $\frac{13}{5}$ and $1\frac{7}{9}$ **BONUS ▶** $4\frac{3}{7}$ and $\frac{14}{3}$

NS6-34 Equivalent Fractions and Division

1. Group the squares to show …

a) six twelfths equals one half $\left(\dfrac{6}{12} = \dfrac{1}{2}\right)$

b) six twelfths equals three sixths $\left(\dfrac{6}{12} = \dfrac{3}{6}\right)$

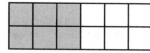

2. Group shaded squares to show an equivalent fraction.

a)

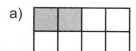

$$\dfrac{2}{8} = \dfrac{}{4}$$

b)

$$\dfrac{6}{10} = \dfrac{}{5}$$

c)

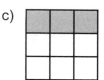

$$\dfrac{3}{9} = \dfrac{}{3}$$

3. Imagine erasing the dotted lines in the first circle. Shade the second circle to show the result and then write the equivalent fraction.

a)

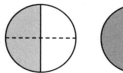

$$\dfrac{2}{4}$$ $$\boxed{\dfrac{1}{2}}$$

b)

$$\dfrac{2}{6}$$ $$\square$$

c)

$$\dfrac{4}{8}$$ $$\square$$

d)

$$\dfrac{4}{8}$$ $$\square$$

e)

$$\dfrac{4}{6}$$ $$\square$$

f)

$$\dfrac{6}{9}$$ $$\square$$

4. Imagine erasing the dotted lines. Then write the equivalent fraction.

a) 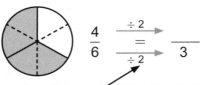 $\dfrac{4}{6} \xrightarrow[\div 2]{\div 2} = \dfrac{}{3}$

This number tells you how many slices to combine

b) 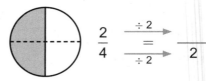 $\dfrac{2}{4} \xrightarrow[\div 2]{\div 2} = \dfrac{}{2}$

c) $\dfrac{2}{8} \xrightarrow[\div 2]{\div 2} = \underline{}$

d) $\dfrac{4}{8} \xrightarrow[\div 4]{\div 4} = \underline{}$

e) $\dfrac{3}{9} \xrightarrow[\div 3]{\div 3} = \underline{}$

f) $\dfrac{4}{10} \xrightarrow[\div 2]{\div 2} = \underline{}$

You can divide the numerator and denominator by the same number to get an equivalent fraction.

Example:　Picture A　　　　　　　　Picture B

$\dfrac{2}{4} \xrightarrow[\div 2]{\div 2} = \dfrac{1}{2}$

Picture A has twice as many **parts** as Picture B.
Picture A has twice as many **shaded parts** as Picture B.

---

5. Use division to find the equivalent fraction or improper fraction.

a) $\dfrac{2}{6} \xrightarrow[\div 2]{\div 2} = \dfrac{}{3}$

b) $\dfrac{5}{10} \xrightarrow[\div 5]{\div 5} = \dfrac{}{2}$

c) $\dfrac{2}{10} \xrightarrow[\div 2]{\div 2} = \dfrac{1}{}$

d) $\dfrac{3}{6} \xrightarrow[\div 3]{\div 3} = \dfrac{1}{}$

e) $\dfrac{15}{10} \xrightarrow[\div 5]{\div 5} = \dfrac{}{2}$

f) $\dfrac{28}{8} \xrightarrow[\div 4]{\div 4} = \dfrac{}{2}$

6. Use division to write three fractions or improper fractions equivalent to …

a) $\dfrac{8}{32} = \Box = \Box = \Box$

b) $\dfrac{27}{54} = \Box = \Box = \Box$

c) $\dfrac{36}{24} = \Box = \Box = \Box$

d) $\dfrac{30}{60} = \Box = \Box = \Box$

NS6-35 Fractions of Whole Numbers

Nick has 6 muffins. He wants to give $\frac{2}{3}$ of his muffins to his friends.

To do so, he shares the muffins equally onto 3 plates:

There are 3 equal groups, so each group is $\frac{1}{3}$ of 6.

There are 2 muffins in each group, so $\frac{1}{3}$ of 6 is 2.

There are 4 muffins in two groups, so $\frac{2}{3}$ of 6 is 4.

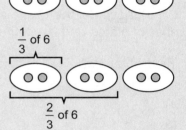

1. Use the picture to find the fraction of the number.

a)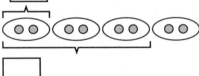

$\boxed{\dfrac{3}{5}}$ of 10

b)

$\boxed{}$ of 12

2. Fill in the missing numbers.

a) $\boxed{\dfrac{1}{3}}$ of 9 = ___3___

$\boxed{\dfrac{2}{3}}$ of _____ = _____

b) $\boxed{}$ of 8 = _____

$\boxed{}$ of _____ = _____

c) $\boxed{}$ of 12 = _____

$\boxed{}$ of _____ = _____

d) $\boxed{}$ of _____ = _____

e) $\boxed{}$ of _____ = _____

3. Circle the given amount.

a) $\frac{2}{3}$ of 9

b) $\frac{1}{5}$ of 10

c) $\frac{3}{4}$ of 8

d) $\frac{4}{5}$ of 15

4. Draw the correct number of dots in each group, then circle the given amount.

a) $\frac{2}{3}$ of 12

b) $\frac{2}{3}$ of 15

5. Find the fraction of the whole amount by sharing the food equally. Hint: Draw the correct number of plates and place the items one at a time. Then circle the correct amount.

a) Find $\frac{1}{4}$ of 8 apples.

$\frac{1}{4}$ of 8 is _____

b) Find $\frac{1}{2}$ of 10 muffins.

$\frac{1}{2}$ of 10 is _____

c) Find $\frac{2}{3}$ of 6 apples.

$\frac{2}{3}$ of 6 is _____

d) Find $\frac{3}{4}$ of 12 muffins.

$\frac{3}{4}$ of 12 is _____

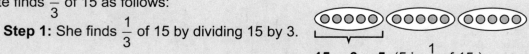

Kate finds $\frac{2}{3}$ of 15 as follows:

Step 1: She finds $\frac{1}{3}$ of 15 by dividing 15 by 3.

$15 \div 3 = 5$ (5 is $\frac{1}{3}$ of 15.)

Step 2: Then she multiplies the result by 2.

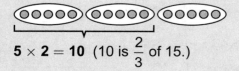

$5 \times 2 = 10$ (10 is $\frac{2}{3}$ of 15.)

6. Find the amounts using Kate's method.

a) $\frac{3}{5}$ of 10 = _____

b) $\frac{1}{3}$ of 9 = _____

c) $\frac{2}{3}$ of 18 = _____

d) $\frac{2}{5}$ of 15 = _____

e) $\frac{2}{7}$ of 28 = _____

f) $\frac{3}{4}$ of 16 = _____

g) $\frac{1}{3}$ of 27 = _____

h) $\frac{1}{2}$ of 14 = _____

i) $\frac{3}{4}$ of 20 = _____

j) $\frac{4}{9}$ of 18 = _____

k) $\frac{5}{8}$ of 24 = _____

l) $\frac{2}{5}$ of 35 = _____

7. Braden gave away three quarters of his 20 stamps.

a) How many stamps did he give away? _____

b) How many stamps does he still have? _____

8. a) Shade $\frac{2}{5}$ of the squares.   b) Shade $\frac{2}{3}$ of the squares.   c) Shade $\frac{3}{4}$ of the squares.

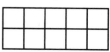   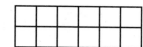   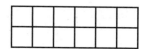

d) Shade $\frac{5}{6}$ of the squares.   e) Shade $\frac{2}{7}$ of the squares.

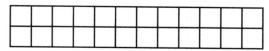   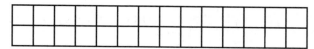

9. a) Shade $\frac{1}{4}$ of the squares.   b) Shade $\frac{1}{3}$ of the squares.

Draw stripes in $\frac{1}{6}$ of the squares.   Draw stripes in $\frac{1}{6}$ of the squares.

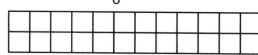   Put dots in $\frac{1}{8}$ of the squares.

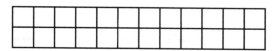

10. Each circle represents a child. Solve the problem by writing "J" for juice and "W" for water in the correct number of circles. The first one is done for you.

a) 8 children had drinks at lunch.

$\frac{1}{2}$ drank juice and $\frac{1}{4}$ drank water.

How many didn't drink juice or water?   _2 didn't drink juice or water_

b) 6 children had drinks at lunch.

$\frac{1}{2}$ drank juice and $\frac{1}{3}$ drank water.

How many didn't drink juice or water? _____

11. 12 children had drinks. $\frac{1}{4}$ drank juice and $\frac{2}{3}$ drank water.

How many didn't drink juice or water? Show your work.

12. There are 20 fish in an aquarium. $\frac{2}{5}$ are blue, $\frac{1}{4}$ are yellow, and the rest are green. How many are green?

13. Hanna has 18 books. $\frac{1}{9}$ are history, $\frac{2}{3}$ are fiction, and the rest are science books. How many science books does she have?

Number Sense 6-35

NS6-36 Division with Fractional Answers

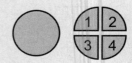

Anton wants to share a pie equally among four friends.

Each friend gets a quarter (or $\frac{1}{4}$) of the pie.

1. Shade how much one person gets. Write the fraction in the box.

   a) 2 people share a pancake equally.

   $\frac{1}{2}$

   b) 3 people share a gold bar equally.

   c) 5 people share a pentagon shape of chocolate equally.

   d) 8 people share a pizza equally.

2. Draw a picture to solve the problem.

   6 people share a pizza.

   How much pizza does each person get? _____

A **unit fraction** is a fraction with numerator 1. Examples: $\frac{1}{2}, \frac{1}{3}, \frac{1}{10}, \frac{1}{57}$

You can use the division sign ($\div$) for equal sharing, even when the answer is a fraction.

Example: When 3 people share a pancake equally, each person gets $\frac{1}{3}$ of a pancake. So $1 \div 3 = \frac{1}{3}$.

---

3. Write a unit fraction for the division statement.

   a) $1 \div 3 = \boxed{\frac{1}{3}}$ b) $1 \div 4 = \boxed{}$ c) $1 \div 2 = \boxed{}$ d) $1 \div 8 = \boxed{}$

   e) $1 \div 10 = \boxed{}$ f) $1 \div 20 = \boxed{}$ g) $1 \div 25 = \boxed{}$ h) $1 \div 100 = \boxed{}$

4. Write a division statement for the unit fraction.

   a) $\frac{1}{6} = \underline{\ 1 \div 6\ }$ b) $\frac{1}{5} = \underline{\hspace{2cm}}$ c) $\frac{1}{12} = \underline{\hspace{2cm}}$ d) $\frac{1}{20} = \underline{\hspace{2cm}}$

   e) $\frac{1}{25} = \underline{\hspace{2cm}}$ f) $\frac{1}{8} = \underline{\hspace{2cm}}$ g) $\frac{1}{15} = \underline{\hspace{2cm}}$ h) $\frac{1}{50} = \underline{\hspace{2cm}}$

Problem: How can 4 people share 3 pies equally?

Solution: Share each pie equally.

There are 4 people, so cut each pie into 4 pieces.

One person takes the shaded pieces.

5. Determine the number of pieces and the number of whole pies.

a) 3 people share 2 pies.

Number of pieces in each pie: __3__

Number of whole pies: __2__

b) 2 people share 5 pies.

Number of pieces in each pie: _____

Number of whole pies: _____

c) 3 people share 4 pies.

Number of pieces in each pie: _____

Number of whole pies: _____

d) 5 people share 3 pies.

Number of pieces in each pie: _____

Number of whole pies: _____

6. Colour one person's share of the pancakes. How much does each person get?

a) 2 people share 3 pancakes.

Each person gets $\boxed{\dfrac{3}{2}}$.

b) 3 people share 2 pancakes.

Each person gets $\boxed{}$.

c) 4 people share 2 pancakes.

Each person gets $\boxed{}$.

d) 5 people share 3 pancakes.

Each person gets $\boxed{}$.

7. a) Draw a picture to solve the problem.

3 people share 5 pizzas.

How much pizza does each person get? _____

b) Is your answer to part a) a proper fraction or improper fraction? _____

Four friends share 3 pies equally. Each friend gets 3 quarters of a pie, so $3 \div 4 = \frac{3}{4}$.

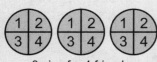 3 pies for 4 friends

 $\frac{3}{4}$ for the first friend

 $\frac{3}{4}$ for the second friend

 $\frac{3}{4}$ for the third friend

 $\frac{3}{4}$ for the fourth friend

8. Write a fraction for the division statement.

a) $2 \div 7 = \boxed{\dfrac{2}{7}}$

b) $4 \div 5 = \boxed{\dfrac{4}{5}}$

c) $3 \div 8 = \boxed{\dfrac{3}{8}}$

d) $5 \div 9 = \boxed{\dfrac{5}{9}}$

e) $5 \div 11 = \boxed{\dfrac{5}{11}}$

f) $9 \div 10 = \boxed{\dfrac{4}{10}}$

g) $10 \div 11 = \boxed{\dfrac{10}{11}}$

h) $15 \div 22 = \boxed{\dfrac{15}{22}}$

i) $23 \div 8 = \boxed{\dfrac{23}{8}}$

j) $32 \div 25 = \boxed{\dfrac{32}{25}}$

k) $43 \div 20 = \boxed{\dfrac{43}{20}}$

l) $173 \div 100 = \boxed{\dfrac{173}{100}}$

m) $19 \div 12 = \boxed{\dfrac{19}{12}}$

n) $88 \div 50 = \boxed{\dfrac{88}{50}}$

o) $56 \div 25 = \boxed{\dfrac{56}{25}}$

p) $67 \div 10 = \boxed{\dfrac{67}{10}}$

9. Write your answers to Question 8 parts i) to p) as mixed numbers.

a) $23 \div 8 = \boxed{2\dfrac{7}{8}}$

b) $32 \div 25 = \boxed{1\dfrac{7}{25}}$

c) $43 \div 20 = \boxed{2\dfrac{3}{20}}$

d) $173 \div 100 = \boxed{1\dfrac{73}{100}}$

e) $19 \div 12 = \boxed{1\dfrac{7}{12}}$

f) $88 \div 50 = \boxed{1\dfrac{38}{50}}$

g) $56 \div 25 = \boxed{2\dfrac{6}{25}}$

h) $67 \div 10 = \boxed{6\dfrac{7}{10}}$

10. Write a division statement for the fraction. Then find the answer.

a) $\dfrac{6}{3} = \underline{\quad 6 \div 3 \quad} = \underline{\quad 2 \quad}$

b) $\dfrac{12}{4} = \underline{\quad 12 \div 4 \quad} = \underline{\quad 3 \quad}$

c) $\dfrac{15}{3} = \underline{\quad 15 \div 3 \quad} = \underline{\quad 5 \quad}$

d) $\dfrac{24}{6} = \underline{\quad 24 \div 6 \quad} = \underline{\quad 4 \quad}$

e) $\dfrac{24}{4} = \underline{\quad 24 \div 4 \quad} = \underline{\quad 6 \quad}$

f) $\dfrac{25}{5} = \underline{\quad 25 \div 5 \quad} = \underline{\quad 5 \quad}$

g) $\dfrac{36}{9} = \underline{\quad 36 \div 9 \quad} = \underline{\quad 4 \quad}$

h) $\dfrac{56}{8} = \underline{\quad 56 \div 8 \quad} = \underline{\quad 7 \quad}$

11. Three friends want to share a 20-kilogram bag of rice equally by weight. How many kilograms of rice should each friend get? Write your answer as a mixed number.

6.666666

NS6-37 Fraction Word Problems

1. The chart shows the times of day when a lizard is active.

 awake but inactive

asleep

awake and active

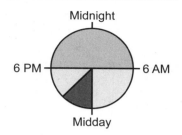

a) What fraction of the day is the lizard …

   i) awake but inactive?   ii) asleep?   iii) awake and active?

b) How many hours a day is the lizard …

   i) awake but inactive?   ii) asleep?   iii) awake and active?

2. Write four equivalent fractions for the amount shaded in the picture.

    $\boxed{} = \boxed{} = \boxed{} = \boxed{}$

3. Steve's dog ate 36 cans of dog food last month. This month, his dog ate $\frac{1}{4}$ less. How many cans of dog food did Steve's dog eat this month?

4. Four families want to share a large 25 kg bag of potatoes. How many kilograms of potatoes should each family get? Write your answer as a mixed number.

5. Anna's backpack weighs $\frac{3}{4}$ kg more than Ravi's pencil case. If Ravi's pencil case weighs $\frac{1}{2}$ kg, does Anna's backpack weigh more than 1 kg?

6. A salmon is $\frac{3}{5}$ m long and a tuna is $\frac{4}{7}$ m long. Which fish is longer? Explain how you know.

BONUS ▶ Dory biked $\frac{1}{4}$ km in one minute, $\frac{1}{2}$ km in the second minute, and $\frac{1}{4}$ km in the third minute. How many kilometres did she bike in three minutes?